MW01251376

Always Learning

THE JUAN ORTIZ JOURNEY

JUAN ORTIZ AND **JUDSON POLING**

Written by Juan Ortiz and Judson Poling

© Copyright, 2020. Juan Ortiz.

Cover design by Tommy Owen
Interior design by Carol Davis, Tree of Life Graphics

ISBN 978-0-9993658-4-7

All rights reserved. No part of this publication may be reproduced, stored in a retrieval system, or transmitted in any form or by any means—electronic, mechanical, photocopying, recording, or otherwise—without the prior written permission of the publisher. The only exception is brief quotations in printed reviews.

Scripture quotations marked ERV are taken from the Easy To Read Version, Copyright © 2006 by Bible League international.

Scripture quotations marked ESV are taken from ESV® Text Edition: 2016. Copyright © 2001 by Crossway, a publishing ministry of Good News Publishers.

Scripture quotations marked GW are taken from GOD'S WORD®, © 1995 God's Word to the Nations. Used by permission of God's Word Mission Society.

Scripture quotations marked HCSB are taken from the Holman Christian Standard Bible®, Copyright © 1999, 2000, 2002, 2003, 2009 by Holman Bible Publishers. Used by permission. Holman Christian Standard Bible®, Holman CSB®, and HCSB® are federally registered trademarks of Holman Bible Publishers.

Scripture quotations marked NASB are taken from the NEW AMERICAN STANDARD BIBLE®, Copyright © 1960, 1962, 1963, 1968, 1971, 1972, 1973, 1975, 1977, 1995 by The Lockman Foundation. Used by permission.

Scripture quotations marked NLT are taken from the Holy Bible, New Living Translation, copyright © 1996, 2004, 2015 by Tyndale House Foundation. Used by permission of Tyndale House Publishers, Inc., Carol Stream, Illinois 60188. All rights reserved.

Scripture quotations marked NIV are taken from THE HOLY BIBLE, NEW INTERNATIONAL VERSION®, NIV® Copyright © 1973, 1978, 1984, 2011 by Biblica, Inc.® Used by permission. All rights reserved worldwide.

Table of Contents

Foreword

YOU HOLD IN YOUR HANDS a special treat from a dear friend. Juan's transparent and witty recap of formative events in his life and the wisdom gained is well worth your investment of time. This life leadership book will inspire and encourage you regardless of your "level" of leadership. In one way or another, we are all leaders. Juan provides practical and actionable insights that can transform your life—if you are willing to step up.

I have known Juan for over 40 years. We met in the fall of 1978 in Wheaton, Illinois, as high school student leaders in a multi-city outreach ministry called Salt Company. Although we went to different high schools and had dramatically different upbringings, we connected—laughed, pranked, roller-skated, joked, and worshipped—several times a week for several years. I looked up to Juan, a year older and decades wiser, in many ways, and still do.

For several years Juan and I were part of a small group that met *early* every Monday morning. I remember lots of energy and laughs as we played off of each other; we were both good at masking our insecurities. During our more serious moments, I would hear Juan's sensitive but evasive prayer request for a family member "in trouble." I may have heard that his father was a problem, but I don't recall much. I do remember that Juan had a huge heart and was genuinely interested in how everyone else was doing.

After college, we had a few brief encounters, most notably when Juan and Becky visited our first apartment in Chicago to sell my wife and me on either body soap or a refrigerator and "the fabulous opportunity to put all our financial worries behind us." As a young attorney at a midsize Chicago law firm, I didn't have a lot of financial worries at the time, and I had very little interest in joining Juan and Becky in their scheme. But we did have a good, albeit short, time catching up.

Fast forward 30 years. Juan spoke at a men's gathering at our church four years ago. He was fabulous, and the story of his childhood was mesmerizing. Thankfully, we reconnected over breakfast a couple of weeks later. Today, we are deeply involved in each other's lives which has given me a unique vantage point and opportunity to learn, encourage, and grow with Juan.

He lives what he teaches. He is the real deal for sure. I hope that you will find some useful nuggets you can apply to your life. But be careful. After reading this, you won't be the same.

David Filkin
C12 Chair, North Shore (Chicago, IL)

Introduction

HURT PEOPLE HURT PEOPLE.

Wounded kids grow up and wound others. People who are mistreated mistreat those around them.

At least that's what the statistics say.

But what happens when forces for good become part of the mix? What is possible when hurt people have something—*someone*—breathing life and hope and new messages of self-worth and intrinsic value into them?

The answer to "what happens" is my story.

My dad was an abusive man, a drug dealer, and a criminal who eventually went to prison. I should have turned out the same. Yet that's not what happened. I beat the odds!

How? This book will tell you. In it are the simple-but-tested, life-changing principles that dramatically altered the course of my life. I not only survived my situation, but I am also thriving.

Read this book, and you'll know how. You'll learn what you can do so the hurts you've experienced don't limit your potential.

It may be that someone you love has been hurt—and is also hurting others. They may be hurting *you*. You want to help but don't know how.

Whether you're dealing with your own hardships or those affecting people you love, let my story inspire and guide you. If a person like me can overcome my past and become successful, it's possible for anyone to experience the same!

All of our lives have chaos, challenges, and regrets. Yet good people around us can gradually undo what bad people did to us. All of us have the potential to become who we dream we could be. But as you'll see from my story, we cannot do that alone. Hope and change come from doing life with other people—the right kind of people. It doesn't matter what happened to you; you can change the direction of your life. You can be different than those who shaped you. I'm living proof of that.

When we're already feeling hurt, one of the biggest enemies to progress is comparing ourselves to others. We look at their lives--how they dress or the things they have--and we feel depressed. The root of so much compounded unhappiness is the sickness called "stare and compare." We already battle messages of inferiority—including envy, jealousy and covetousness—that leave us feeling even more "less than."

But there is another reason to watch others closely: we can learn from them and be inspired. Other peoples' successes can show us our *potential* and improve our *position*. It's actually a good thing to invite others into our lives to help us, mentor us, and sometimes even correct us. But if you do that—and I believe you should—don't let yourself get caught up in the comparison game. Focus on what you can do to better your life. Become the best version possible of *you*—not someone else.

This book is filled with real stories from my life. I explain key principles I learned so you can benefit from them, too. I hope these lessons will encourage you and challenge you to think and act differently. If you are willing to try just a few of them, you will change the direction of your life. I'll even go out on a limb and promise if you make these principles consistent habits, you will be able to live the life you've always dreamed of.

Once you start to change and have success, you will become a person of influence. It seems to be a universal law that as people rise, others rise with them. If nothing else, you will be asked what you did to become such a success. You might be asked to give public talks about it, and maybe one day you'll be persuaded to write a book about it.

That is what happened to me.

I feel the need to warn you, though. Part of this journey to a better life means dealing with your hurts. Things have happened to all of us that keep us from being all we can be. It's not easy dealing with those hurts, which is why so many of us end up being "carriers" who infect others. But there is another side to hurt called healing. It's a place where pain is processed, not passed on. Where wounds are cared for, not ignored. Our sufferings become lessons we learn, not lead-weights we labor under. We can pass beyond them—not pass them on.

You will need to build a community of people to help you. You might even need to see a therapist. I did, and I'm grateful for how much value I got from that. Above all, you'll need mentors--men and women who give you direction. You must find trustworthy people and regularly seek their wisdom.

And right here, right now, I offer you this message of hope: if you are willing to read this book, learn these principles, and apply them to your life, your life will change for good!

So turn the page and let's get started. A better you awaits…

Section One

Building Self-Image

If you're prepared, you're able to feel confident.

—*Robert J Ringer*

The more you love yourself, the less nonsense you'll tolerate.

—*Author Unknown*

You deserve the love you keep trying to give to everyone else.

—*Author Unknown*

Fear not, for I have redeemed you; I have called you by name,
you are mine…you are precious in my eyes, and honored,
and I love you…

—*God (Isaiah 43:1, 4, ESV)*

Homecoming

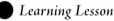

Learning Lesson
Stay focused until you finish and accomplish your goal!

THE STUDENTS IN THE GYMNASIUM HUSHED as the announcer spoke. "And this year's Homecoming King is...Juan Ortiz!"

The school assembly burst into applause.

I was shocked. True, I knew that because I was on the football team, my classmates had all heard of me. I also knew I had a well-deserved reputation for being funny and being a trickster who knew how to play a practical joke on people (sometimes even teachers—which really made me popular and often got me into trouble).

But I was really surprised to be elected Homecoming King. My senior class was filled with cool guys. Did my classmates choose me as a joke? Was this just another way I was being mocked?

My self-image was not the best in high school. I was frequently berated throughout grade school. So by high school, I was a mess. When the outside voices weren't physically present

High School Homecoming Court

criticizing me, I had mental recordings of all that chatter playing on repeat in my head.

I grew up with an abusive dad—a drug-dealing, wife-beat-
ing, child-shaming monster. We were a family of Mexican
immigrants, who for a time lived in a dilapidated, abandoned
farmhouse with no heat or running water. In fifth grade, when
I first came to the Chicago area, I didn't know enough English
to understand what was going on in my classroom. My teacher
made me sit in front of the class and apart from the other kids.
He wanted me to feel appreciated, but I felt like I was on dis-
play like an animal in the zoo—a curiosity for all the other
kids to watch.

My boyhood felt like the epic story of an outsider always
looking in. I constantly wondered what it would take to become "normal" like all the other kids. The American culture
they understood so well was a mystery to me.

For several years, most of what my siblings and I wore came
from boxes of donated clothes. My grooming habits were
minimal—I had no clue that I even smelled different than the

other kids. I tried to observe how the "cool" kids acted, but so much of what they did that gave them that status didn't even register with me.

The day before my first day of eighth grade, my siblings and I were going through one of the boxes of donations given to us from a benevolent church in the area. We were trying on the clothes and sifting through all the castaway junk people had given. I found a jar of Dippidy-do, a styling gel for women. I had no idea what it was. My mom saw the label and said, "Oh, I think that goes in your hair." So the next morning as I hurried to get ready before the bus picked us up, I scooped out a dollop of the sticky goo and smeared it in my hair. *Now I'm cool!* I thought. I stepped off the bus—certain that everybody would notice the dapper-looking guy gliding down the side-walk. And notice me they did!

There I was, brown pants that were too short, a yel-low-checkered shirt that clashed, and white socks with black shoes. My mom had buttoned up my shirt all the way to the top. And to complete the look, I sported a wide, white leather belt.

Of course, some of the kids snickered at me and mocked me. But I thought I had changed for the better. I thought for sure I was going to be a stand out stud—accepted and ad-mired as one of the cool kids. *Even the Dippidy-do didn't work? I thought. They're still making fun of me!*

In my earlier years, I just stood quietly while kids teased me. But I had gotten bigger since grade school. Now I was in junior high, and I wasn't going to just take the ridicule. So I pushed around a couple of kids who mouthed off at me. "El Dorko, the Latino Bully."

And overnight, I became a fighter. Why wouldn't I? I watched my dad punch my mom, and I knew what it felt like for my dad to punch me. I knew that no kid could possibly hurt me as bad as my dad did. I learned to take the punishment at first, then later how to power-up. When anyone tried to take me on, I destroyed them. I definitely had a reputation: "That Juan kid is crazy!" Still, some of the guys respected me. Eventually, the bad guys started leaving me alone. I'm sure they said stuff behind my back, but I made them regret it if they were foolish enough to say it to my face.

Now here I was, four years later, elected Homecoming King. Playing sports had helped me become popular, and I had finally learned how to dress. My sense of humor blossomed; I found that if you can make people laugh, they are willing to overlook so many of your peculiarities. On the football field, I was "one of the guys." Out there, I could hit other boys hard—and get pats on the back for it! I found my aggressive nature—all that pent-up rage from abuse from my dad—gave me a fighting spirit that I could channel into action on the field.

Unfortunately, my newfound fame started going to my head. And my football coach, Jim Rexilius, taught me an important lesson during that Homecoming game.

High School buddy, Keith Cote

Though he didn't mentor me in any formal way, Coach Rex had a lasting impact on my life. Everybody wanted to play for Jim Rexilius; he was a local sports legend. The athletic field at Wheaton North High School is named after him. He sported a military-style crew-cut and was a no-nonsense motivator. He didn't tolerate kids goofing around, or smoking, or any of that kind of behavior. He was a firm disciplinarian, and I loved him because I needed that in my life.

Coach Rex knew I was from a troubled family, but he was still tough—in a good way. He didn't favor me. He didn't give me breaks. He said, "Ortiz, you'll earn it like everybody else." But I respected that, and I always felt love for Coach Rex. I felt like he cared about me.

Coach Rex led a Fellowship of Christian Athletes group at his house. I started going as a freshman with my friend Keith Cote.

Cote helped me with a lot in my life. We met in eighth grade, and he became the friend who showed me the ropes. He taught me about sports and showed me how to play. He taught me about what people were like. He showed me the basics of life. We also had our faith in common. What's ironic is that now he actually oversees the Chicago chapter of the FCA.

I remember watching as Coach let more mature students play important roles in the FCA meetings. Some really cool seniors stepped up to lead. But I would always watch Coach, especially when he led us in prayer. It moved me to see a strong man who had such a simple and vibrant faith.

Every Friday, all of us football players would wear our jerseys to school because we played our games on Friday nights. It's one of the coolest parts about being on varsity. I was a good athlete so I was on the field a lot; sometimes I'd even start.

At the Homecoming game, I was excited to get out on the field. But Coach didn't put me in. I didn't understand, and eventually asked him what was wrong. He said, "You're not playing tonight, Ortiz. Your head is in the wrong place."

"What do you mean, Coach?" If anything, I felt like being Homecoming King made me more pumped to play.

"This whole Homecoming King thing has gotten to you, and I don't respect it. You need to focus, son. Tonight is about football, not about recognition. All that rah-rah crap is going to your head. You don't have the right motivation."

I wasn't on the field for a single play the entire night. It was so painful.

Privately, I sat on the sidelines tears stinging my eyes, though I did my best to not show anybody my emotions. All my friends asked, "What's wrong? Why aren't you playing?" Even afterwards, some of the alumni who knew me from previous years sought me out. "What happened tonight? You're one of the key players. Why weren't you in there?"

All I could tell them was, "Coach didn't want to play me."

To this day, telling that story makes me sad. And to this day, when my wife, Becky, hears it, she gets upset. She feels it was abusive—like Coach Rex was too harsh and didn't understand me. I'm glad my wife sees my heart and wanted Coach to value that as much as my performance. (To this day, Becky is very protective of how people treat me.) But I feel like he was a man of principle, and as that kind of man, he knew I needed to focus on the task in front me; if I couldn't do that, I forfeited the opportunity to play.

Though it's a hard story to tell, today the overall effect on me from that experience is positive. I took away an important lesson: I frequently ask myself the question, "Where is my mind right now?" I need to know if I'm in the game—or just using the game to get something else. Am I focused on what I need to be doing today, or am I just seeking attention? Do I want results or applause? Do I want coworkers to like the good we do, or do I want them to like me and think I'm good?

Maybe if he could do it all over again, Coach Rex would let me play. He might see he went a bit too far in making me sit out the whole game. But it doesn't matter, because I got the learning I needed from it. I do not hold it against him. He did what he thought best. And based on all the other good things he did for me and the overall fairness and decency of his character, I can't believe he intended to hurt me.

At the end of the year at the senior banquet, Coach Rex gave me an award for being the best leader. That meant a lot to me. I still have the little five-by-seven inch plaque that says, "Wheaton North Football 1979 Best Leader." He saw my potential, not just on the field but with my teammates. He encouraged me to lead the pre-game team charge: "All right, Ortiz, get them going!" I'd jump in the middle of the guys and get everybody hooting and hollering. Coach loved it. He saw my energy, and though he didn't say it, he probably thought, *Wow. OK. That kid is not the greatest player, but he does have a gift of inspiration!*

My lasting impression of Coach Rex is that he loved the tough-to-love kid. He knew something of my weird family situation. My dad showed up drunk at that Homecoming game—and it wasn't the first time he did that. Dad was particularly obnoxious that night and got arrested. It was halftime. I was on the track as Homecoming King, and my dad got into a fight in the stands right near where I was standing. Coach Rex saw that, and hung with me. He frequently encouraged me and spoke well of what he saw in my character. At Fellowship of Christian Athletes meetings, he often put his arm around my shoulder. He did enough things to make me feel like I was a winner. He was a role model of what a tough-but-caring leader could look like.

After I left for college, Coach Rex invited me back to speak to the teams he coached. As I did that, I started to see my potential to be a communicator, which is now an important part of my life. And one time after I spoke, he took me aside—keep in mind he was not an emotional or sentimental guy at all—and he said simply, "Son, I'm very proud of you. You're a good person." And that was all he said to me. It was all he needed to say.

Learning Lesson Recap
So many times we start well but do not finish what we set out to do. It's important to remember to fulfill all our responsibilities in order to complete our work and achieve our objectives. A coach, friend, or someone we trust can be an enormous help to keep us focused on the task ahead.

Remember
Stay focused until you finish and accomplish your goal!

For which one of you, when he wants to build a tower, does not first sit down and calculate the cost to see if he has enough to complete it? Otherwise, when he has laid a foundation and is not able to finish, all who observe it begin to ridicule him, saying, "'This man began to build and was not able to finish."
(Luke 14:28-30, NASB)

Pranks

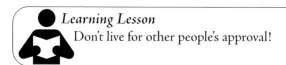

Learning Lesson
Don't live for other people's approval!

TWO WEEKS BEFORE MY FRESHMAN YEAR in college, my dad went to prison.

Truthfully, I wish he had gone a lot sooner. All my life, dad was in trouble. He was often involved in drug deals, fistfights, and even shootings. He had a stash of guns—obtained illegally—that could arm a platoon. He physically and emotionally abused my mom and us kids. It took my mom decades to finally stand up to him. Thankfully, with the help of a neighbor, she finally reported his abuse to the authorities.

Going to college was a big transition even apart from my dad's incarceration. I was at a school barely 40 minutes away, yet it felt like I was abandoning my mom. Being the oldest of six kids, I never thought I would leave home at all. I assumed I would care for my mom and my siblings my whole life—even more so with dad completely out of the picture.

I was so unsure of myself. I barely made it through high school. I felt stupid and out of it. In fact, the only reason I

Tim Geoffrion

applied to college was because of the insistence of my youth pastor, Tim Geoffrion, who believed in me and told me I could do it.

Tim loved me and my family. He regularly came over to our house and spent time with us when no one else would—admittedly, we were kind of a rough crowd. He helped us with homework. He talked with my mom and dad. Many times, he stayed and ate dinner with us. And I don't know how he did it, because he was a student at Wheaton College at the time, but sometimes he would even buy us pizza for dinner. He always shared God's love with us. He was a true example of a disciple of Jesus. Tim is founder and president of Faith, Hope and Love Global ministries and is still in my life today. For the past 10 years, he has been a spiritual mentor.

I arrived at the dorm that first day, not knowing anybody. Fortunately, the college lifestyle made it possible for me to shine. Living with suite-mates helped me get in with some guys right away. My high energy and humor was very well received. My stories and jokes worked like magic to make me popular. Right away all my suite-mates were impressed with me: "Oh my gosh, this guy is so much fun!"

Most freshmen I got to know loved to play pranks on each other—especially on girls we liked. The more pranks I played, the more people liked me and thought of me as the life of the party.

What they didn't know was that behind the scenes, I struggled with fear. I felt pressure academically and financially. On top of that, I often felt inadequate as a young man. Childhood messages from my dad still haunted me. I knew he was wrong to criticize me and certainly wrong to beat me. But almost two decades of his influence didn't go away just because he wasn't around anymore.

I did what a lot of people do when they come from an abusive background; I kept up the outside image and did crazy stuff to get attention.

Some of my pranks went too far. I'm not proud of it. I was trying hard to be liked. The pranks also showed how insensitive and immature I could be.

One of my jobs during freshman and sophomore years was working in the college cafeteria. I say "one of my jobs" because I held down three at the same time: In addition to working in the cafeteria, I worked as a busboy at a local restaurant and delivered furniture donated to the college. My job at the cafeteria was to clean the dining hall and kitchen at night when everybody was gone. One of the advantages of working there was helping myself to some of the food. I took cookies and soda—not a lot, but it was still nice to have free food in light of how I'd grown up in such deprivation.

I made friends with some missionary kids who grew up in Africa. They had a big pet snake, and they fed it all kinds of weird stuff. Sometimes they'd go to the pet store to buy him a rat or some mice, but a lot of times they found frogs in our local pond and fed those to the snake.

One day they called me. "You've got to see this frog we caught!" It was huge—probably three times the size of a normal frog. They were going to feed it to the snake.

When I saw it, I said, "Guys, don't put it in with the snake. I got a better idea."

Mind you, these were very conservative missionary kids who never got into trouble and rarely did anything that might look like being rebellious. They were curious but concerned. "What do you want to do?"

I said, "Here's what I'm thinking. I have access to the cafeteria, and I bet we could play a great prank using this frog."

At about 11 o'clock that night, we snuck into the cafeteria. I went into a walk-in refrigerator. Inside, there were several giant salad bowls—huge bowls full of cut-up lettuce ready to serve the next day, covered with Saran Wrap. So I peeled the Saran Wrap off of one of the salad bowls, and we put the frog down in the bottom of the bowl. We were surprised because it just sat there in the bottom of the bowl and didn't try to jump out. We pushed the lettuce back over the frog until we covered it completely.

We could barely sleep that night thinking about how funny it was going to be the next day when they brought out the salads. At lunch, we sat as close as we could to the salad bar. There were a bunch of us there, waiting.

Cafeteria workers brought out a couple of salad bowls, and nothing happened. I started wondering if maybe someone found the frog earlier and let it go. The third bowl came out, and they unwrapped it. Again, nothing happened.

But just then a girl reached into that third bowl with tongs and...boom! The frog jumped out. The salad bowl looked like it was exploding, lettuce flew all over the place.

The girl shrieked, and some of the kids nearby looked like they were going to get sick to their stomach. This gigantic frog jumped all over the other food laid out on the salad bar. At first, no one could catch it.

We were dying laughing. I'm sure a lot of people suspected me having something to do with this.

The manager finally came out, caught the frog and got rid of it.

Soon after, I was called into the Dean of Students.

"Juan, we think you had something to do with the frog in the cafeteria today."

I confessed. "Yeah, I did it. A friend caught the frog and was going to feed it to his snake. When he showed it to me, I got the idea to put it in the salad bar. He had nothing to do with it other than catching the frog."

The Dean wasn't amused. "What is wrong with you, Juan? What is your problem?"

"I don't know. I thought it would be funny. I didn't think there would be any harm."

Other than a stern warning, there were no other consequences.

The frog incident made me a legend among my classmates. My buddies told the story to others. The tale got bigger and bigger with each re-telling: "You should have seen it: the frog was as big as a dog…and it ate a loaf of bread…it picked up the salad tongs and threw them across the room…it practically bit a kid's hand off." I never corrected them. It felt good to be at Christian college and break the rules and become well-known for it.

I'm not suggesting that was OK. But there was something in me, in those other kids—and I suspect in all of us—that wanted to do something "out of bounds" from time to time. Something in us all can cause us to bend rules or even do something against our morals just so we can be liked or accepted.

No one knew what was going on inside of me. No one knew about my abusive background, my fears, and the insecurity I lived with every day. When I did those wild, out-there pranks, I temporarily forgot all that inner turmoil. I'm sure I used that feeling like a drug. I understand why people get drunk or use other substances to numb their pain. There is another, better way to cope with all that, but I do understand why so many choose to take the easier route.

Other pranks had more serious consequences.

On a Sunday night for no particular reason, a bunch of us from my soccer team got to talking about playing hooky. "We don't want to go to class tomorrow. How can we get them to cancel school?" We brainstormed how we might be able to shut down the school for a day.

As we colluded, an idea emerged.

Trinity was a small school, and there was one main building where almost all classes were held. We knew if we could some-how make that building temporarily unusable, they wouldn't be able to hold classes.

At the end of one hallway was a two-story atrium that opened to both floors. The upper floor was administration offices and the lower floor was classrooms. One of the guys had a key to the building—not sure why—and at 1 a.m., we all snuck in the building and started sliding desks and chairs out of the classrooms into the hallway. Then we slid all that furniture down the hallway to fill the atrium area, right up to the doors. We took every chair and desk—anything that wasn't bolted down—from all the first-floor classrooms and packed the atrium. We even stacked chairs and desks upon other chairs and desks, so that it looked like the barricade in *Les Miserables*.

When our pile of furniture was almost halfway up to the balcony that overlooked the atrium, we went up to the second floor and started going through admin offices and conference rooms taking stuff out of there and piling those items on top of the pile we started below. Not only was the floor space covered, but it reached up to the balcony railing.

That's when we really got carried away—and destructive. Instead of carefully placing chairs and tables on top of the pile, we carelessly tossed stuff over the second-story railing onto the other furniture below. How we never got caught making all that noise, I'll never know. But as we were doing that with abandon, we ended up breaking some of the chairs and desks. We didn't know we were doing damage, but we should have suspected all that rough handling of furniture would at least have left dents and dings.

When our pile was all the way up to the second story railing, we snuck out the back door. We knew that anybody trying to get in those main doors would be met with an atrium jam-packed with furniture. There was simply no way to get in other than back doors that students weren't supposed to go through. And it would take the custodial staff many hours—if not the whole day—to reset all the things we moved.

Like the night before the frog prank, we had a hard time sleeping because of the anticipation. We kept laughing and thinking about the reaction everybody would have the next day.

The next morning, students, teachers and administrators were all gathered around the entrance unable to get in. Just to show how stupid we were, we also thought it would be funny to come to class carrying lawn chairs! "Hey we heard that something was up with the chairs today, so we brought our own. I wonder what happened with all that furniture?"

We weren't just playing dumb; we were *actually* dumb!

The Dean immediately pulled us aside. "Okay, you guys. This is your doing, isn't it?" This time the missionary kids got in trouble, too. "You knew this was wrong, but you went ahead and did it."

The students loved it. Classes were cancelled for the day so they could put the building back together. We found out later that we damaged some of the chairs and tables. I felt bad about that part, but I loved all the attention we got. Everyone knew we did it.We didn't have to tell anybody. We were getting a reputation:"What's the next crazy thing Juan and those guys are going to do?"

We knew vandalism was wrong. But even though we didn't mean to do harm, our prank was destructive. The damage we did cost the school. Most teenagers like us only think of the fun they'll have when they act like that. That single focus blinded us to the other consequences of our actions.

Another time, about 20 of us guys picked up a little parked car and put it on the steps leading up to the academic building. They had to get a tow truck to lift it off and get it back on the street. We also went up on the roof of the library and used rolls of toilet paper to write some words up there. It wasn't anything obscene. But when it rained, it left a sloppy mess that wasn't easy to clean off.

As I look back on all those pranks now, I know there was a lot going on inside of me emotionally. I was driven by the hurt I always felt and the currents of bad self-esteem. I didn't care what the administration thought of me, because I wanted my friends to think I was cool. I hadn't yet made the connection that as a Christian, inner peace and satisfaction come from seeking God's affirmation. My friends couldn't offer that. I now know that at any age, living for other people's approval is a form of idolatry. And making anything more important than God always leads to dissatisfaction.

I don't know how many fines I was assessed, but I had a lot of them. The desks prank was especially expensive. Even then, the financial consequences wouldn't dissuade us. We'd go right back out and do other pranks.

It all came back to haunt me years later when I had to face a choice my son made.

 Learning Lesson Recap
We can waste a lot of time and energy trying to gain the admiration and approval of friends and people we look up to. It's okay to want people to like us, but that can't be our sole focus. And when we have fun or do things to make people laugh, it shouldn't be at their expense. Too often we spend money we don't have, on things we don't need, to impress people we don't even like. It's important to live true to ourselves, not conform to the whims of what others want us to be.

Remember
Don't live for other people's approval!

Do you think I am trying to make people accept me? No, God is the One I am trying to please. Am I trying to please people? If I still wanted to please people, I would not be a servant of Christ.
(Galatians 1:10, ERV)

Section Two

Personal Growth

Success…seems to be connected with action.
Successful men keep moving.

—*Conrad Hilton*

I'm a greater believer in luck,
and I find the harder I work, the more I have of it.

—*Coleman Cox*

And let us not grow weary of doing good,
for in due season we will reap, if we do not give up.

—*The Apostle Paul, (Galatians 6:9, ESV)*

3

Like Father, Like Son

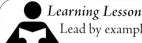
Learning Lesson
Lead by example because people are watching you!

THE PRANKS I PULLED IN COLLEGE mostly seemed like fun. At the time, I didn't realize all that was going on inside me that motivated me to do them. I got some great insight into all that about 15 years later. At that time, I was married to my college sweetheart, Becky, and we had three kids.

I got a phone call from the principal of my son's junior high school.

"Mr. Ortiz, there's been an incident with your son, Steven. You'll need to pick him up and take him home. He's been suspended for three days."

When I got there, I found out Steven decided to pull his own prank. A bunch of his friends threw money at him and dared him to streak. So he jumped up on the gym stage and took off everything but his boxers. Some teachers told him to get down. Steven jumped off the stage but started running. They chased him, and he knocked down some kids accidentally. He also knocked over a table.

The big soccer star and his cheerleader girlfriend

My wife and I were so disappointed. Becky wondered aloud, "What have we done? This is terrible. We must be lousy parents—why else would he be like this?"

My next thought was, *Well, it kind of reminds me of me!* But I didn't say that.

Then she asked, "What are we going to do now?"

"I don't know."

"Well, for sure we have to ground him. And no TV for a while."

I agreed.

I knew Steven and I had to have a talk. I prayed for wisdom.

I began by putting his actions in a moral perspective, "Steven, this is not acceptable behavior."

"I'm sorry, Dad."

I continued. "This doesn't represent our family well. We take pride in doing God's will, and this does not reflect that value."

"I don't understand your behavior. Why did you do this?" It wasn't just a rhetorical question—like I was shaming him indirectly. I really did want to know, and I wanted him to know the motivation behind his acting out.

Steven had a ready reply. "Dad, I've heard you tell so many stories about college and high school and all the fun pranks you did. I just wanted a story of my own. I wanted to do something that someday people would laugh and go, 'Remember when Steven Ortiz did that?'"

Silently I thought, *Oh, good for you, Juan! All those stories you've been telling—now your son's trying to get your reputation!*

Becky sat there trying not to laugh even though she was still mad.

"Well, that's true, Steve. That's my fault. I only talk about the funny side of those stories. I can see why you would want to do something like that."

We then sent him to bed.

When he was gone, Becky pointed out the obvious. "This is your fault, you know. You did all those things in college, and you brag about them."

I couldn't deny it. "Well, they were kind of fun. You laughed at them, too."

As we were talking, my other son, Philip, came down. "Dad, is Steve in a lot of trouble?"

"Yes, he is. He's grounded for a long time."

Philip waited a long moment before he spoke, "You know, he's like the most popular kid now. Everybody thinks he's the greatest!"

I remembered how that worked!

Philip continued. "Can I ask you one question?"

"Sure, son."

"You *do* think what Steve did is pretty cool, don't you?"

I smiled. "Yeah, I suppose it is kind of cool. At least he didn't hurt anybody."

Philip smiled. Even Becky broke into a stifled grin.

"But don't let him know that I said that!" I added sternly.

Let's go back to where I left off telling the story of my life in college.

By my junior and senior years, I started to calm down. I wasn't as crazy as I had been during the previous years—particularly my freshman year when I was so out of control. I'm sure a lot of young men go through a phase like that.

I began to change when I started to care more about what God thought about me. It was a spiritual maturing that happened gradually over the next 10 to 15 years. It seasoned me and helped me become a better version of myself. I wanted to be kind because I saw that God was kind. I wanted to do good for others because that's what God does for us.

One of the most positive influences during those final two years of college was having Becky in my life. We met and started dating in college, and she was very grounded. She helped me

Becky, Philip, Juan and Steven

with my low self-esteem, and she caused me to become more responsible in general.

Ironically, many people were not happy she was dating me. People actually came up to her and told her—warned her— that I was no good for her. "You cannot marry this guy, Becky. He has a lot of emotional problems, a lot of damage. You could date anyone you want. So many guys are attracted to you. Move on. Juan may be funny and outgoing, but long term, he's trouble." And they were right.

But Becky believed in me. She saw the core of who I was underneath all the external acting out. Even though she was very popular and could have had her pick, she picked me. Maybe it was God influencing her. I don't know. But Becky always said—and to this day reminds me: "I know you love people, Juan. I know you love God. The one thing I always see in you is that you don't want to disobey God."

Another positive influence during those years was Coach Schartner, my soccer coach. In him I saw a man who was

Juan, with coach Schartner standing in the back ground

Trinity College Soccer Team 1985

funny, who told jokes, and even did some pranks, but he never hurt people. He refused to mock people. There were times in a meeting when he said, "Hey, stop! No more joking. We need to be serious." He could downshift (and help us do that) instead of always staying in overdrive like I was.

Even after a reprimand, he'd come back and put his arm around me. Speaking like a caring father, he said, "You know why I had to tell you that, right?"

I knew, and said, "Yeah, I was disrupting the meeting."

"That's right. And you're a leader, and I want you to lead."

I was team captain for two years for him—my junior and senior years. He really helped me to control myself.

"As a leader, as captain, you're the example. People look up to you; they watch what you do all the time. Everything that comes out of your mouth, your actions—all those things are important."

Sometimes, I would open up to him. "Coach, I feel like I'm a failure. I feel like I can't lead. Maybe you made a mistake."

"No, Juan. I didn't make a mistake. You're the captain. You're our leader. Hang in there."

Coach Schartner is still in my life. He still believes in me. He's so positive and builds me up. The thing I love most about Coach is he always hugs me.

What a contrast to my upbringing. My dad belittled me. He shamed me. So often in public, he embarrassed me. But in college I had people in my life who built me up. Coach Schartner, my friends, and Becky were really "for" me.

From time to time, Becky would say something that hurt my feelings. She was very up-front and direct in her communication, and I often took that wrong. Even though she just commented on a small matter, I felt embarrassed and over-reacted in response. I'm ashamed to have to admit I behaved horribly in those situations with anger, rudeness and sarcasm.

Thankfully, Becky knew how to stay calm. She said, "Okay, what hurts? What just happened? Because you have made a turn." She knew how to talk to me without getting pulled into my drama herself. She also had good counsel for me: "Look, Juan, when you're hurt, you need to learn how to deal with it. Otherwise, you end up hurting other people. I know you care about people; I know you don't want to hurt people; I know you love God. Yet when you get hurt, you change and become really mean."

Like Becky, Coach Schartner also tried to help me get past my overreactions. "You're better than you know, Juan. You have a great heart. You're a good leader. You care about people." He often challenged my self-doubts. "You are better than you think you are." He wasn't talking about soccer—he meant as a person. He wouldn't let me feel sorry for myself. He wouldn't let me make excuses. And he would always be positive with me.

I built some great friendships, and those guys loved me and had a huge influence on me while I was at Trinity. Bob Southworth was a consistent example of focus and hard work. He helped me a lot with my school work. I probably wouldn't have graduated without Bob! Plus, he was very patient with me. I could never wake up for my morning classes. He was always my alarm. And I also used to steal his quarters to do my laundry.

I eventually paid him back—30 years later!

Kevin Olsen, "KO," has been a leader in my life since college. He has always been a dreamer and a confident, driven person. He always pushed me to be better—he's still doing that for me today.

Dan Dondit was another roommate of mine, but only for one semester. I had many roommates over the four-and-a-half years of college. It might have been because I was hard to live with! Dan was a great athlete, so we were always competing. We played soccer and basketball together all four years in college. Dan was always our top player—in basketball, he was an All-American, and still holds records at Trinity. Dan taught

Jamming along to some fun music;
(From Left:Juan, Jimmy Kline, Kevin Olsen and Dan Dondit).

Danny Vandixhorn, Soccer team mate

me to be competitive. He showed me by example to believe in myself and always go into a competition believing I could win.

Danny VanDixHorn was my basketball coach's son and my roommate during my last years in college. We were a lot alike: we played soccer, we laughed together, we loved music, but most importantly, I could talk to Danny about anything. Danny came from a great family, who lived close to Trinity. I got to know his family, and I really came to love them. His mom and dad were so loving to me in a difficult time of my life. They are what I believe godly parents are supposed to be like. Danny was just like them—loving, kind, and giving. More than anything, Danny was always there for me. To this day, it brings me to tears when I think of how much that family did for me. And Danny is still in my life. Amazing.

All of my friends were such encouragers. They helped me understand my intrinsic worth. They would say things like, "You're good. You have a good heart. You love the Lord. You don't want to hurt people. You can lead. You help others. You inspire others." Those were the words that, even now, I talk about in my life.

I wasn't popular with everybody, and not everybody was good to me. Many kids disliked me. Some of the more conservative students saw my sarcasm, my tantrums, all the pranks I did my first two years at college, and judged me: "You're not here because of the Lord or his will. You don't care about God." Based on the things they saw me do, I understood why they thought that.

I was never really violent when I got angry, but I was rude and mouthed off. One time in the dining hall, this kid—a Bible major—was sitting at the table next to me and he said something that hurt me in front of several of my friends. Everybody kind of laughed because it was sarcastic and silly.

I was so humiliated. I went ballistic. I got up, went over to his table, and sat down across from him. "So you're a Bible major? You're going to go change the world because you're amazing, right? You're an amazing individual. Because somehow you're blessed and God called you to be a pastor, right? Because why? Are you smart? Oh, yeah, you're really smart. Look at you. You can't button your shirt, but you know how to preach to people, right? So let me ask you a couple questions. What does the Bible say about losers like you? You think you're going to be a pastor and lead the world? Because you're such a great example and your parents are so proud, right?"

He apologized. "Alright, already! I'm sorry I said that."

"No, no. You're not sorry. See, that's what pastors do. They walk by other people and they look down their noses at them. Oh, great example! You're an amazing Christian leader! God's gift to the world. Hey—why can't you look at me? Pastors look at people. You can't look at me. How are you going to be a pastor?"

"I'm done. I'm leaving." He stood up.

I stood up too. "Yeah, you do that. You just leave. Where are we going now, huh? You want to go somewhere else and talk about it? Or do you want to put your nose in the Bible and forget about the rest of us peons who don't measure up to your greatness?"

Finally some of my friends grabbed my shoulder and tried to calm me down. Other people around us actually got up and left because of how inappropriate I was being. Though I didn't swear, I was rude and sarcastic. I wanted to make him feel like crap—and I was pretty good at it. He finally just left, which is the only reason I finally stopped talking.

Later, one of my friends confronted me. "Juan, you were a total idiot back there." It killed me to hear that. My good friend's disapproval crushed me.

I tried to defend myself. "That guy was rude to me."

"All he did was make a sarcastic remark to you. But you went off on him. You were crazy. Maybe he shouldn't have said what he said, but you were an idiot."

I was broken. "I just…I guess I have a problem, don't I? I'm not well."

Teachers also got in my crosshairs. I remember nodding off one time in history class. The teacher came over and rapped on my desk to wake me up. Startled, I barked, "What are you doing?"

"Waking you up. Nobody sleeps in my class."

"Oh really? Well, do your job right, and maybe we wouldn't fall asleep!"

He was understandably upset, but I didn't relent. "What's wrong? Can't handle students? What are you doing teaching college, then? Sorry, but we're not all perfect like you! You think you're better than us, don't you?"

Even as those words came out of my mouth, I felt bad. I knew it was wrong, but I couldn't control my emotions.

The teacher told the dean, "I will not teach Juan Ortiz. He can't be in my class." I had to drop that class because he refused to put up with me.

I remember my dad doing that kind of thing in public. He berated my mom and us kids. He was rude and critical. For a while during my high school years, he attended church with us. But even then, he stood up during a prayer meeting and questioned the pastor. In Bible studies, he interrupted and challenged what the leader was saying. He'd make people feel inferior and never admit he was wrong—about anything. If my dad came to my school or to sporting events, he criticized people. When he got drunk, he was an absolute jerk; that's when he turned violent and got into fights.

Even though I wasn't physically abusive like my dad, I could hear in my voice the echo of his. I knew if I was going to live the way I wanted to, I had to find a way to make it stop. But I didn't have a clue how.

Learning Lesson Recap
Leadership is influence, and that gives us power. We can use that power to build up people or hurt them. Every day we lead and influence others; we must use that influence to accomplish positive things and help change lives for the better.

Remember
Lead by example because people are watching you!

Imitate me, as I imitate Christ.

(1 Corinthians 11:1, GW)

4

Sarcasm

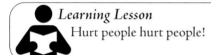

Learning Lesson
Hurt people hurt people!

IT HAPPENED AGAIN.

I went off on a fellow-student, teacher, or teammate and embarrassed myself. I hurt someone because I couldn't control my sarcasm.

At times like that, I sank into serious depression. I'd drive to a park and just weep. I despised myself.

Sometimes, I retreated into my dorm room and locked myself in. I didn't want to be around anybody. I'd sit in my room crying, angry at myself. The last thing I wanted to be was like my dad, but here I was, sounding just like him. My friends came to the door, but I wouldn't let them in. A suite-mate knocked: "Juan, I'm your roommate. I have to come in!" Then Becky came to the door. "Juan, what's going on? Come out. We need to talk." I heard my roommates tell her that I hadn't gotten out of bed for two days. I was so depressed.

This kind of behavior continued for years after college. Becky and I got married right after my senior year. I went off on her verbally so many times. I was vicious. Why she stayed with me, I don't know. It breaks my heart to have to recount the stories about how I behaved back then.

I suppose the one thing I did right was admitting I was out of line very soon afterward. Becky saw how devastated I was once the dust settled. I was so broken every time I went into one of my sarcasm rants. I knew I was in the wrong, and I always came back and apologized. She didn't excuse it, nor was she willing to allow me to stay stuck there. But when I made progress, she encouraged me. I have so much respect and appreciation for her because she continued to be patient and see the best in me despite my outbursts.

Right out of college, I landed a job in downtown Chicago. It lasted only six months. Yet in that short time, that job impacted me in two lasting ways.

First, I learned discipline. Because I worked downtown, I had to get up at 6 a.m. every day. Then I would drive to the train station in Deerfield to catch the 7:10, which got me into the city by 8 a.m.. I would walk to One South Wacker, where my office was located. Work started at 8:30, and I was late many times. Eventually, I was able to arrive consistently on time. Learning to be responsible made me feel important, even though I didn't have an important job. It just felt great to be working in a corporate environment.

The second big impact was meeting Teresa. Little did I know that she and her boyfriend Jeff (who later became her husband) would become great friends of ours. Teresa was sharp, beautiful, and really funny. From day one, she said, "I can't wait for you to meet Jeff. You're gonna become best friends!" And she was right. Jeff Conrady is more than a friend. He's like a brother to me. He has helped me with my relationship with Becky, with my finances, and with making major decisions in my life.

Jeff & Teresa Conrady

I left that corporate job to help start a church called Ginger Creek. My primary job there was working with the youth. But among my other responsibilities, I ran the adult men's sports' leagues. I remember getting kicked out of games for my angry outbursts and being belligerent. I wasn't physically abusive, but I was certainly not a model leader.

When we held a basketball tournament at Wheaton College, one of my younger brothers played on the same team. He was even angrier than I was, and he got into an argument with another player. I went to break it up, and the other player called both of us some terrible names. Enraged, my brother went after him physically. When I pulled him off, they were both ejected from the game.

As the other guy was leaving the court, I followed him. I would not stop berating him. I followed him out of the gym and called him every name in the book. "You're a loser. You're a weenie. You can't handle this."

He couldn't believe it. "Dude! What is your problem? I'm leaving. Back off." And while he walked away, I still kept at him. I couldn't control it.

When I finally quit yelling and came back into the gym, the coaches told me, "You can't play any more."

What do you mean I can't play? I organized the league!"

"We don't care. You're out. Don't come back into the gym."

I again took a walk of shame. *I work for a church, and this is how I act? What kind of a leader am I?*

At times, the despair turned into suicidal thoughts. *I'm such a loser. I'm never going to change. Better to just end it than keep living and having these out-of-control episodes. What good is it to know God loves me when it doesn't keep me from letting him down? I'm better off dead and in heaven than alive and hurting people on earth.*

I talked to Jeff who was becoming my best friend. Jeff and Teresa got married and we bought condos about 50 yards from each other. We lived there for over seven years. We have so many fun stories of our time together there. And even though those were great years and great memories, I was always dealing with depression and suicidal thoughts.

The irony is I believed suicide would be the ultimate act of disobedience and I didn't want to let God down in that way, too. So I never got to the point of actually making a plan. I felt hopeless, but I also knew ending my life would be the supreme slap in God's face. If I did that, I'd be saying he was the One who gave me the gift of life and this is how I repay him.

I've reflected a lot on how I got to that point in my life. I see that my sarcasm and anger had roots in my past. It was never going to work just trying harder to be less critical. Even though I was a Christian and had God's love and power in my life to help me, I needed to understand my story in order to change it.

The most obvious contributing factor was my dad. He was my model of manhood, and it was a terrible example. I've written in detail about many of the things he did in my previous book, *Never Forsaken: The Juan Ortiz Story*. Suffice it to say, he was violent and abusive, and no kid should have to put up with that kind of treatment.

Yet a strange sequence of events led to my copying his anger and sarcasm in my adult life—even though I hated it (especially when he aimed it at me).

It began in junior high. At first, I tried to be funny without any anger or bad feelings toward another person. I was just trying to get people to like me, and it worked. Kids would say, "Oh, my gosh. That kid is hilarious!" And the more people thought I was hilarious, the better I felt about myself.

I thought, *Wow. This is pretty cool. They like me.*

But then I would take it too far and feel guilty as a result. I felt conflicted, but not enough to stop. It didn't take long before I turned pretty ugly.

I remember a heavyset girl who went to our church. We ripped on her, and she didn't seem to care. Everybody made fun of her even though we knew she had a lot of dysfunction in her background. We'd say to her face, "Why are you so fat? You're disgusting."

Eventually, she became promiscuous. Who could blame her for wanting boys' attention given all the abuse we heaped on her? I remember thinking, *What is wrong with me? Why am I being so mean? I'm part of the reason she's so messed up!* But teasing her was a way to fit in with my friends, to make her "the other" so I wasn't "the other" any more.

It's a classic way humans create pseudo-community: find a common enemy—a common lesser-than person or group—and make them bad or weird so you can feel accepted by your own group. Create a "them" so it's clear who "we" are. Everybody needs to know who is in the clique so get specific about who is outside it.

It's what I saw my dad do. He mimicked people, made fun of them, and verbally berated them so he could feel superior.

The only difference between my father and me was I didn't swear or get physically violent. When Dad got really angry, he'd hit people. I didn't do that. But I was still my father's son when it came to the sarcasm, the mimicking, the putting people down, and making fun of them.

As the years went by, I refined my technique. In high school, I was the class clown. I was funny and also rude.

My psychology teacher in high school had a weird name and an odd voice. I made fun of him all the time. One day as he taught us, he said to the class, "Let's talk about what a 'deviant' in society is. I think a classic example would be our very own Juan Ortiz."

The entire room laughed. And I laughed, too. I thought, *OK…I have no idea what the word deviant means, but he called me a deviant, and everybody laughed. I guess I'm a deviant. Ha-ha!*

Then I found out the definition of the word deviant. I tried to brush it off: *Whatever! I don't care what you call me. You're a loser!* But inside, it hurt. I never showed the pain I felt having someone in a position of authority call me that.

He also said to the class that I was the kind of kid who would never do anything with his life. He was wrong to say that, but I was wrong to behave the way I did. I kept teasing him and ended up failing that class because I was as rude and disrespectful as you can get.

We had another substitute teacher once named Mrs. Hicks. I decided to call her "Bag-of-Tricks." When she called my name during roll call, I said, "Here, Mrs. Bag-of-Tricks."

The whole class laughed. She scowled at me, not believing what she just heard. "What did you say?"

"Nothing. I just said I was here."

Many years later, I spoke at an event, and Mrs. Hicks came up after my talk and greeted me. "Hi, Juan. It's so nice to see how you turned out."

I didn't recognize her at first. "How do I know you?"

"I was a substitute teacher in your high school."

I still couldn't place her. "Oh, really? What's your name?"

"I'm *Mrs. Bag-of-Tricks.*"

I cringed inside but forced a weak smile. "Oh, yeah. Mrs. *Hicks.*"

"Well, well, well! You *do* know my name!" she said wryly.

Though she was able to laugh at it later, I imagine, at the time, I hurt her just like I hurt so many people.

Another way I learned to get attention was to mimic people. I copied their actions and mannerisms, and sometimes even sounded like them. I studied them, watching all the subtle and not-so-subtle things they did and said. Friends were blown away by my impersonations. I always picked the peculiar and weird things about people. If they had a limp, I'd do that. One security guard at school had a fake eye that wandered and looked in a slightly different direction than the other one. I did this bit where I pretended to get caught by him but kept moving around because I didn't know which eye he was looking at me with.

I kept up the mimicking routine even into adulthood. Though I was more sensitive, I still did it without thinking of the consequences. One time I did it in an executive meeting. My boss pulled me aside and said, "Do not do that—don't mimic people."

I said, "I'm just goofing around. I don't mean anything by it."

"Even if you think it's funny, it's humor at someone else's expense. If you want to make fun of someone, make fun of yourself. But not others."

I got the message.

At times like that, I was totally self-absorbed. I was on a covert mission to get people to like me and think I was great. I was trying to feel normal to cover up my broken insides. When I found out I could get people to laugh, that became my go-to method for getting attention and what I thought was love. The paradox was, the way I tried to get love and acceptance was to make other people feel bad. I know that doesn't make sense. But it took me years to change.

One of the big problems of our day is domestic abuse. People who are supposed to love each other can do horrible things to each other. Often it has its roots in how someone unconsciously copies what they saw growing up in their own family. We mimic the behaviors we repeatedly witnessed throughout our childhood—even though we vow to be different. When we feel powerless or embarrassed or hopeless, we lash out. This is especially true of men, but many women relate to doing this as well.

The solution is not to shut off our emotions or become passive. What's actually needed is assertiveness training. When people learn how to use their power to get what they want in healthy, direct ways, they aren't as likely to lash out. We hurt people when we're frustrated and we don't know what else to do. But when we feel powerful, we have nothing to prove. We know we have options. When we find ways to get what we want by asking and negotiating, we won't resort to violence—or in my case, verbal abuse.

That was the paradox of my life for many years: I wanted acceptance so badly that I was willing to hurt people to get it.

Ironically, we can turn all that rage and hatred we have for others against ourselves. I think some of my depression was actually me beating myself up. If we can't get what we want, we are willing to destroy people to try to get it. And sometimes the person we destroy is ourselves.

Substance abuse is another way we try to numb the pain of feeling bad about ourselves or feeling powerless. We act out or use even to the point of self-destruction.

Someone has said, *If you don't transform your pain, you'll transmit it.* I hadn't learned to transform my pain at that point, so I was transmitting it—gift-wrapped in humor and sarcasm.

I needed to learn to be powerful and direct without being hurtful. It's OK to speak your mind, but you also have to learn to be kind and aware of the effect you have on others. I've been on that long journey most of my adulthood. And I'm glad to say, I've made a ton of progress.

Learning Lesson Recap
Words can build up, or tear down; they are simply a reflection of what is in our hearts. When we are hurt, we often say things that create more hurt. To change our words, we must change our hearts. And we can do that only by dealing with the hurts that have built up inside us.

Remember
Hurt people hurt people!

A good man brings good things out of the good stored up in his heart, and an evil man brings evil things out of the evil stored up in his heart. For the mouth speaks what the heart is full of.
(Luke 6:45, NIV)

5

A Winning Environment

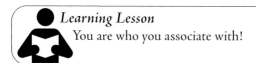

Learning Lesson
You are who you associate with!

I LOVED BEING A YOUTH PASTOR. Having a focused mission and purpose was life-giving to me. It was a great fit for my temperament, and every day I looked forward to meeting with kids, preparing messages, and working with a great team of volunteers. True, earning only $14,000 a year was tough, but Becky had a good job, and we lived very simply. We did that for three years. It was great.

People tell you when you have kids, your life will never be the same. But you can't really know what they're talking about until you have your own baby. When we had our first child, I was blown away by the seismic shifts that shook our world.

Our son Steven was born in 1988. To say that life changed would be a huge understatement. Becky didn't want to put Steven in daycare—she wanted to be home with him. So she left her full-time job to be a full-time mom. She babysat a few kids at our house, but that didn't come anywhere near replacing her former income.

We both loved Steven and were excited to be parents. I agreed fully with Becky choosing to stay home with him. But now I had a dilemma. I wanted to support my growing family, *and* I wanted to be a youth pastor. Working in ministry didn't pay enough. So I had to make a choice. In order to provide for my family, I had to leave youth work and find a better-paying job.

What to do? Though I worked odd jobs as a kid, I had no marketplace experience. I had no idea what my strengths were. I knew I was funny and quick-witted. I was great with kids. And, I was a master at being sarcastic. Not exactly a stellar list of marketable strengths!

Right about that time, Bob Southworth called.

"Hey, Juan. I recently got involved in a business that I think would be a good fit for you."

Bob was a CPA, so I knew he was smart. But I thought any kind of business he wanted me to consider was surely above my pay grade. "Bob, I'm not really a business guy. You know that, right?"

He answered, "I know that's not your forte. But this business is something just about anybody could do. It's mostly about hard work, not education or expertise."

I said, "If you're doing it and you think I can do it, I'm in. You know business—I don't. I'm just a dumb kid."

"Don't sell yourself short, Juan. You have a lot of abilities, and I think this would be great."

My wife was standing in the kitchen and overheard the conversation. "Hold on a second, Juan. What is he talking about? I want to know details. Give me the phone," she demanded. After I handed it to her, she said, "Bob, what's going on?"

I could see her defenses go up. I'm sure Bob could hear it in her voice.

"Hi, Becky. Don't freak out. My wife and I want to come over with a friend to show you guys a business opportunity."

"Well, what is it?" she asked.

"We'll tell you when we get there."

"No, Bob, you're not coming over until you tell me. What is it?"

While she talked, I whispered, "Becky, who cares? Let's just do it."

Becky was pretty sure it was a direct sales marketing deal and wanted nothing to do with it. At the time, she thought it was a scam. "Bob, if it's direct sales, we're not interested."

He said, "Well, it is. But I think you need to look at it. You can always say 'no' afterward."

"We're not interested." She handed me the phone thinking that was the end of it.

"Uh, Bob. Tell you what, come on over anyway. If Becky doesn't want to do it, that's fine. I'm happy to listen." And I hung up.

You can imagine the conflict that caused!

(By the way, Bob told me later when he made that phone call, it went exactly as he thought it would. He knew I would say "yes" right away and Becky would have a problem with it!)

Bob came over with his friend, Gerry Betterman, and made the presentation to both me and Becky. I actually enjoyed it. I was excited and ready to do whatever Gerry and Bobby told me to do. So I signed up that night.

Even though Becky was not happy, she did agree to support me. I think in the back of her mind, a little flicker of optimism allowed her to imagine: *It would be nice if we could make some extra money.* We really did need it—we were broke.

Gerry then told me he would be back in one week to share the same presentation. He said, "I'll be here next Tuesday at 6 p.m. Try to get as many people as you can to come and hear the same presentation you guys just heard tonight."

Gerry and Sharon Betterman

I was so excited at the possibility of getting lots of people involved in the same business. According to Gerry and Bob, there was a decent amount of money to be made if I did that.

Gerry gave me a few steps to follow—what I would later come to know as "The Pattern" for how to have a successful meeting.

He gave me a script that told me what to say to people as I invited them. He then asked me to build a list of family, friends, and anyone I knew. Last he gave me a few tapes to listen to. (This was the 80s so there were no CDs, cell phones or YouTube videos.) The tapes were stories from people who were successful in this business. I listened to them that night.

I put together a list of about 20 names. I told Gerry I didn't know any more people. But that wasn't true. When I showed the list to Becky, she saw I had a lot of fear—a fear of rejection. Because I was afraid, I didn't write down everyone I knew. Instead, I listed just a few people, ones I thought were a "sure thing" for getting involved. She knew that if this was going to work, I needed a much bigger list. So, with Becky's help, we came up with the names of over 100 people.

I started making calls the next day. I decided I could talk to people without using the script Gerry gave me, but the few people I asked said "no" right away. One person warned me that this kind of business was a scam and I should get out of it right away.

I was discouraged. But I didn't tell Becky or Gerry that I wasn't going to do it anymore. I just didn't make any more calls. I figured I would call Gerry the night before the meeting to cancel and then quit.

My driven, strong wife noticed my lack of effort. "Why haven't you been making calls?" she asked.

"I'm not going through with it," I answered.

"Why?" she asked.

"Nobody wants to do it," I countered. "It just doesn't work like Gerry said it would."

"Well, how many calls have you made?"

"Ten, I think."

(I exaggerated—I'd actually made three.)

She looked at me suspiciously. (It's uncanny how Becky picks up on it whenever I stretch the truth!) "Really, Juan? You made 10 calls?"

"Well, no, not exactly. But one of the guys I talked to warned me about this organization. He told me it wouldn't work the way they said it would."

Becky replied, "Look, that guy might be right. But I think we need to give this thing a try before we give up."

"'We'? You mean, like, you and me?" I asked.

"Yes. I want to help. I think if we do it together, we have a better chance of success."

With Becky's help, we both invited people and had our first meeting. Only three people came, but one of them was very interested.

Right away, Gerry booked a meeting at that guy's home. Gerry suggested Becky and I talk to more people—along with this new guy—and hold another meeting next week there. He gave me a few more tapes. I listened to them right away.

We started making more calls. One couple that came to the next meeting were our good friends Jeff and Teresa Conrady.

Jeff was in rare form at that first meeting. He made a bunch of sarcastic remarks about the business being a scam. He kept interrupting Gerry and making jokes the whole time. I was sure he was going to say "no" when presented with the opportunity to take part. I was also concerned this might get between us as friends and he would make fun of me for being so gullible.

Becky was upset with Jeff for how he was acting during the meeting. She believed this could work and that Jeff was just being rude.

It's amazing to see the difference in our self-image back then and how it affected our resolve. I was afraid of rejection and ready to quit when someone said "no" to us. Becky became more determined to build it in spite of people saying "no."

Much to our surprise, Jeff and Teresa said "yes!"

Despite his joking around, Jeff saw the potential. He knew this could be something big. Like Becky, he is a confident and driven person.

Jeff's enthusiasm completely turned me around. I got excited again, and recommitted to put my whole heart into trying to make it work.

In an ironic turn, the couple who hosted the meeting—who were originally on board—decided that night not to continue.

Gerry saw Jeff was a "Go-Getter" and started personally working with him. Gerry did a meeting or two for Jeff and that was all the coaching he needed. After that, Jeff started to show the business plan himself.

Gerry recommended I present "The Plan" to people, too, but I told him I couldn't do it. I didn't think I would be very good at it.

Becky encouraged me to try it and offered to help me. And so we started to do our own meetings and show The Plan.

Within 30 days of Jeff and Teresa signing up, they had 30 people in their group! Becky and I only had four or five (outside of the two of them). I felt stupid and was ready to quit again. But Gerry reminded me my group included all of Jeff's group; all 30 of his people were in my downline (every person under me).

Gerry continued to give me motivational tapes. He also gave me a book, *The Magic of Thinking Big*. I was not a good reader, but I did want to learn. And wow—once I got into it, that book opened my eyes to some new ideas I had never thought about before.

Jeff set an example for me of hard work. Once he made a decision, he never looked back. Instead of me leading him, he led me. Jeff filled me up and encouraged me. And he loved to make me laugh. And from time to time, he also really loved to really scare me, too! (To give you an example, one time he sat in my bushes in front of my house and jumped out at me when I got home. We lay there on the ground for the longest time trembling—me from fear, him from laughing.)

I was so up and down—excited one day, ready to quit the next. Because of my bad self-image, I just could not stay positive. It was as if all Gerry's encouragement was poured into a sieve; it just drained out after a while because there was nothing solid in me to keep it in. But he didn't stop encouraging me. He kept giving me tapes and books. By continually creating a mentally positive environment, some of the teachings started to stick. Eventually I bought my own tapes and books because I could see the value of consistent input and how it was helping.

Dan Smith

Gerry invited us to attend a seminar at the end of the month. He said there would be several hundred people there. A very successful couple, Dan and Betsy Smith, would share their story and their knowledge of how to build this business.

The tickets for the event were $20 per person. Becky and I had almost no extra cash, so I felt like we could not go. However, Becky thought it would be a worthwhile investment.

"Let's go see what these people have to say. If their advice helps us, the increase in our business will more than pay for what the tickets cost."

Becky knew that to be successful you needed to invest in your business. This was a learning opportunity and we needed to make the investment of money and time. (It would take up a whole Saturday for the drive and seminar.)

We loved it. Dan and Betsy were amazing! We had a chance to meet them afterwards. I didn't realize it then, but they were to become important mentors for us.

Ortiz's and Conrady's, Direct Sales Convention

In addition to hearing Dan and Betsy speak, many people were publicly recognized for their achievements. I didn't know until then that there were different levels of success you could attain.

Much to my surprise and delight, this was one of the most inspiring environments I ever encountered. I was learning new ideas and encouraged to put them into practice. Real people were doing the same, and we were all gaining from each other's successes.

Jeff and Teresa from our group also came to the seminar. Then and there, they resolved that at the next event like this, *they* would be among those who walked across the stage and were recognized.

And that is exactly what they did!

Thanks to Jeff and Teresa's hard work, Becky and I would also walk across that stage to be recognized. The growth of their business unit pushed us to that first level of recognition as well. It was so fun to work with people we liked and get a payoff together.

After that seminar, many people knew who we were. We were like celebrities—at least locally.

Several months later, we were invited to attend an even bigger event out-of-state. More than 1,000 people were expected. The cost was $100 per person. There would be more recognition for us, and we'd hear from some of the biggest leaders in the business tell their stories of success. Man, I could not wait.

We bought our tickets, and, when the time came, we made the eight-hour drive with our group. The event was amazing! I was overwhelmed by the inspiration of everything I experienced. I met lots of people and learned so much. We were also recognized as up-and-coming, new leaders.

The biggest thing I gained was a sense that I could have all my dreams come true. These seminars infused my hopes with a sense of inevitability—if I kept at it, I *would* achieve success. As an extra carrot dangled in front of us, they announced a promotion to give us even more incentive to build our business: whoever hit the level of sales they specified by the end of that calendar year would receive an all-expenses-paid trip to Hawaii. That was like throwing a steak in front of a hungry dog—I was pumped!

During that event, Gerry arranged for Becky and me to spend some more time with Dan and Betsy Smith, whom we'd met at the earlier seminar. During the few hours we met with them, Dan went through what he called "The Pattern" of how to build the business. He also showed us what he called "The System" of how to keep people in the business.

Until then, I didn't realize that those who succeeded had a consistent and disciplined way they operated. The power to grow this business was through duplication. If you could duplicate what you were being taught and pass it on to your downline so they could do it, too, then everyone would win.

We started showing the plan to more and more people. Our confidence and skill at sharing it grew. When people weren't interested, we didn't lose any momentum. We just thanked them for their time and went on to the next prospect.

Becky and I were both excited and completely involved. We truly believed we could make all our dreams come true! We also had about 10 couples showing the plan under us. And we had more and more people showing up to events with us, which allowed us to be recognized more. Though the added income from the business at our current level was modest, we hoped that, if we kept at it, we would see the fruit of all our efforts.

Eleanor Roosevelt is credited with saying, "Great minds discuss ideas; average minds discuss events; small minds discuss people."

To its credit, the direct sales environment was overwhelmingly about ideas. We learned about so many new concepts that we could apply to our lives to make them better. No one had ever taught me these things.

We also expanded our network of friends and acquaintances; we met people from all walks of life. They, too, were growing and learning in this positive, success-focused environment. I continued listening to tapes and reading books, hungry to understand what I needed to do and how to stay motivated at doing it. I couldn't get enough.

For the first time in my life, the possibilities seemed unlimited. As I faced my fear of rejection, I found that keeping my dreams and goals in front of me every day changed my pattern of thought and quieted the negative internal messages. I knew it wasn't happening by chance. By controlling what I thought about, I could control what was happening in my life. The future I wanted was within my grasp if I would simply apply myself.

Becky and I both started to write down our dreams. We got pictures and put them up so we could see them. We even went out to touch some of our dreams. We test drove new cars, walked through houses that were for sale, and tried on clothes we hoped to buy someday.

We dreamed of one day being able to give more money to the church and help non-profit organizations. Our dreams weren't just about us becoming rich; they were about having choices and resources to be more generous. Success was being free to do what our hearts really wanted to do. For us, that meant someday making a big impact on people's lives through giving, speaking, and maybe even writing a book or two.

At 26 years of age, I hadn't known many really successful people. But now, I was meeting so many of them and was learning from leaders of all ages and from all fields of knowledge. Many of these great people are to this day still my friends.

Even more importantly, I was able to build relationships with several men who became—and still are—mentors in my life. In addition to Dan Smith and Gerry Betterman who I already told you about, I became friends with Mike Jakubik.

When I met Mike Jakubik in the direct sales business, I realized this was a special person. I had heard him and his wife, Lynn, speak several times. I was inspired by their story, and I loved the way Mike spoke. He was clear. He was direct. But what I loved the most is that he was funny. I wanted to speak like him. I wanted to be like Mike. I just wanted to be his friend. Today I talk to Mike three to four times a week, even though we live in different parts of the country. He is still one of the key mentors and advisors in my life. Mike, Lynn, Becky and I are all very close friends. Our kids have grown up together, and we consider each other family.

All these men—Dan, Gerry and Mike—have taught me so much about marriage, kids, and finances. I cannot think of

Mike and Lynn Jakubik

anything important in my life that I have not at some point talked about with at least one—and usually all—of these men.

A very important idea I first heard about through a talk given at an event was finding balance in life. The speaker had us imagine a wheel. He said that the middle of the wheel, the axle, is the thing you value most in life. For me, that was my relationship with God. He drew several spokes around the wheel and said each one of them represented a different area of our lives. He mentioned faith, family, friends, finances, fitness, fun, and a few others. He pointed out that if you neglect one or more of these spokes, your life becomes out of balance, like a bicycle wheel missing some of the spokes. No amount of success in one makes up for not having success in the others. They are all important and necessary to true balance and fulfillment in life.

Since hearing that speech decades ago, I've been studying that concept. I read many books about balance, purpose, personalities, temperaments, and desires. I worked with people of all ages, and all that experience helped me develop my own version of this concept. It is what I call "The Core Balance System." (I'll have more to say about that later.)

I consistently use this concept in my life, and I teach it to others to help them. It is a powerful tool that grew out of being exposed to so many success principles, successful people, and a positive, uplifting environment. I will share a lot more about the Core Balance System in a later chapter.

My story of coming from poverty and an abusive upbringing to now having positive self-esteem and a chance for success made me a sought-after speaker. Together, Becky and I gave talks all over the country and even internationally. Recordings of my personal story and some of my teachings were circulated literally around the world.

None of this would have happened if I had not become a student first. I needed to change. I did that by studying the business and slogging away at the work. I also needed to overcome my fears. At first, I was afraid to speak in front of people and to show the plan. But I must have presented that plan several thousand times in living rooms here in the U.S. as well as in other countries. Doing something that many times cured my fear.

This business environment gave me an opportunity to hear stories from successful people and rub shoulders with true winners. But most importantly, it opened doors to develop some great relationships with mentors. Those people are still helping me work toward achieving my dreams. They also protect me from any dead-end roads I might be tempted to take. My advisors keep me on the straight path that leads to true meaning and fulfillment.

Do you want to change your life for the better and reach your potential? Then consider the people you associate with. Because what they are, you will become!

❖

Learning Lesson Recap
It's a simple fact of life that we become like those we hang out with. If we want a better life we need to spend time with better people. Who are our friends? Who do we follow? Who are our heroes? It's important to take stock of who we admire and who gets our attention because we will most likely end up just like them.

Remember
You are who you associate with!

Whoever walks with the wise becomes wise, but the companion of fools will suffer harm.

(Proverbs 13:20, ESV)

6

Mexico

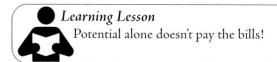

Learning Lesson
Potential alone doesn't pay the bills!

THE DIRECT MARKETING BUSINESS was an amazing training ground. It helped me gain confidence and fueled my drive to succeed. But after I left youth ministry, I couldn't make enough money at direct marketing to pay the bills. So while we stayed involved building that business, I was always doing other jobs.

For at least 15 years, I worked three jobs. I volunteered for 20 hours a week at the church. I put in what seemed like 50 hours a week in direct sales. I worked at about 10 different full-time sales jobs in an effort to land a steady job I liked. I constantly felt overwhelmed. I had little control over my time, and I always felt like a total failure.

What helped me during these years were my friends and mentors. Being neighbors with Jeff and Teresa helped us survive those years. We saw each other nearly every day and spent every weekend together. Jeff was a great source of encouragement. He was confident in himself and in life, and that rubbed off on me.

He's also been incredibly generous. Once, when we were really strapped for cash, he bought me four new tires because we could see the steel bands underneath the rubber.

Jeff has taught me how to have fun and not take myself so seriously. No one else in my life has so consistently made me laugh. He's almost as funny as Teresa (who is almost as funny as I am). Jeff has brought me so much joy in my life!

Another person who's brought enormous value to my life is Abe Doncel. We met when I worked at the church. He was a volunteer staff member, serving alongside me doing youth ministry. Decades later, we still do ministry together.

Perhaps my oldest friend in life is Tom Dowling ("TD"). I've known him since we were both 15 years old. TD and I are as close as friends can be. Our kids have grown up together. He is the most honest, real person I've ever met. I can count on TD to speak the truth to me. He's the kind of guy who gets in my face, with love, and tells me what I don't want to hear, but need to.

Underneath what everyone saw on the outside during those years, I still felt a lot of fear. In that season of life with all my changing jobs and the direct sales business not paying off as much as I'd hoped, finances were a big part of what I worried about. But so many things were new or unfamiliar. All of them caused me stress.

Being a new parent was a huge source of fear as well. Our first boy, Steven, had come along, and, like many new parents, I had no idea how to care for a baby. I wasn't sure how to be a good father. Remember, my dad was a terrible example.

Because I was afraid, I didn't even try to help Becky with "baby stuff." She got up at night with Steven, changed his diapers, fed and rocked him, and basically took complete care of him. I felt bad about not getting up at night or doing the other things to help, but I was overwhelmed. I doubted myself and every move I made.

I felt like I was drowning. Between new parenting jitters, financial pressure, and lack of steady employment, I was not doing well. I must have quit 10 jobs in those first five years after leaving youth ministry. It was awful. I bounced through a few different sales jobs, mostly straight commission. None of them lasted.

A year and a half after Steven, our second son, Philip, was born. Our family was growing. Yet I was still trying to figure out how to provide for my family. And there was an ache in my heart to find the bigger purpose of what my life was supposed to be about.

I tried being a headhunter but stayed there only eight months. I also worked for a uniform company for a year or so. When firemen and policemen needed their uniforms, they'd get issued a voucher, and we sold them uniforms. It wasn't really sales; it was more just filling orders. That didn't last either. I also delivered packages for over a year. I got to know Chicago like the back of my hand and literally wore out my tires. This is when Jeff bought me the tires.

Although our direct marketing business kept us busy, it wasn't making as much money as I had hoped. We were in no position to do it full-time. What really kept me going was doing talks at the events sponsored by those who were in the business. It was a lot of fun, and they paid me. I already discovered I had a knack for public speaking while I was a youth pastor. I used my humor and extroverted personality to motivate and inspire people. I got to be well known, which felt like success. But we still struggled financially.

Eventually, one of the higher-ups in the direct marketing business asked me if I wanted to help him start up the business in Mexico. Since my family is from Mexico, it seemed like a good fit. It sounded like a great opportunity to get in on the ground floor of a new market. Becky and I were excited about it.

There were a few drawbacks. He paid me very little—other than expenses. After taxes, it was not enough money to pay our bills. But he sold me on the idea that I would be an exclusive distributor in Mexico, which seemed to have potential.

I learned a painful lesson, however; "potential" doesn't pay the bills.

I went back and forth to Mexico for over a year. Those were really difficult trips for me. A lot of times they'd send me by myself, and I was insecure and emotional and lonely. Becky stayed home by herself with our two little boys. We got deeper in debt and went through painful marital struggles.

When we first got married, a friend helped us purchase the condo in Wheaton (the one near the Conradys) with no money down. Living there was costly, and we were still struggling with debt. During that time, Becky's parents lived in Massachusetts. They decided to do a mission trip for about six months, to Afghanistan. They knew we were struggling to make ends meet, and they wanted to help.

"What do you think?" asked my father-in-law. "While we're in Afghanistan, you could live here. It's completely furnished—you could just move right in."

"That would be great," I replied.

"You need to pay utilities. But other than that, your only expense will be food."

It was such a fantastic opportunity. We sold our condo in Wheaton, moved to Massachusetts, and paid off our debt.

What we didn't realize is that we owed the IRS money. Because of how naive we were about finances, we hadn't been setting aside quarterly payments on all the self-employment income we had. When the IRS caught up with us, we had a huge bill, plus penalties and interest. We reached out to a friend and an accountant, Mike Whalen, who got us on a budget and negotiated a payment plan with the IRS. Mike not only helped us through that, he became a great friend. He's still doing our taxes decades later.

I still traveled frequently to Mexico, leaving Becky home alone. Even though our financial picture started to get a bit better, I still struggled to make my life work.

One trip during that time was to Guadalajara, Mexico. It's on the west coast, right on the ocean. My boss told me he set up two or three meetings with people who were interested in joining the business. So I went down there to give presentations and get them involved.

My boss paid for my airfare. But then he threw me a curveball. "Juan, why don't you pay for the hotel with your credit card? Then, when you get back, I'll reimburse you. I'm over in Australia, and I just can't do it right now."

I figured as long as he paid me back before I had to make the credit card payment, we'd be fine. I agreed and flew down to Guadalajara for two nights and three days.

The first meeting was set up at my hotel. But the guy never showed up. I was discouraged and overwhelmed. Even though I'm Mexican by ethnic background, it was an unfamiliar culture. It was a foreign country for me, and I was completely alone. That day, I wandered the streets of Guadalajara, asking myself what on earth I was doing. Doubts crowded my mind. How was I going to earn a living? Was doing direct sales actually going to work out?

The next morning, I got up and decided to start my day with a trip to the exercise room. I tried to do some of the little things—my routines—to push back the fear and panic that lingered. I was supposed to have a meeting for lunch then do a larger meeting for a group of people later that night.

Nobody showed up for lunch.

I thought, *Are you kidding me? I fly all the way to Mexico just to get stood up.* I felt like I was in a desert walking toward a mirage. As soon as I got to what I thought was an opportunity, it dissolved.

Get a grip, Juan. Look, the big meeting is tonight. It will be okay. There should be 10-15 people there. That will make this trip worth it.

I was back in my hotel room when the guy who was hosting the evening meeting called me.

"Hey, Juan, I'm sorry to do this to you, but nobody was interested."

Stunned, I said nothing.

He continued. "I know we were going to have you over for supper before the meeting, but since no one's interested, I think we should just cancel the whole night."

I finally spoke. "Listen, since I've flown all the way from the U.S., why don't you and I meet for supper anyway. I could explain more about the business."

"Nah, that's OK. I don't want to waste your time. The more I think about it, I'm really not that interested in doing this."

I had been there two days and didn't have a single meeting. The only conversation turned out to be a cancellation. I was all by myself. This was before cell phones or the Internet, so texts and emails weren't an option. I couldn't just call my wife without incurring significant international, long-distance charges.

I was so discouraged and depressed. My flight was not until 1 p.m. the next day. It had been a rough 48 hours and I still had to endure another empty, wasted day.

The next morning, I went to the lobby to check out.

"Did you enjoy your stay, Señor Ortiz?" the clerk at the front desk asked.

"Si, it was great. Bueno," I lied. It wasn't their fault I was miserable, and I didn't feel like getting into it with him.

"And would you like to leave the room charges on this card?"

"Yes, that's fine." I waited while he ran the card.

He came back with a troubled look. "I'm sorry, but there's a problem with your card. Do you have a different card? For some reason, this one isn't working."

I called the toll-free number on the card. They said I had plenty of credit, so the card should work.

I thought, *How could this trip get worse?* Then it did get worse.

True to my pattern, embarrassment led to sarcasm. I'm doing a lot better with that now, but, at that time in my life, I was still rude and easily allowed myself to get out of control. Embarrassment really hurt, and I covered that pain with anger. I felt scared, too, but I wasn't going to show that, so I got even angrier.

I argued with the desk clerk. They brought in the manager, and I argued with him. I got louder and more combative.

"I just called my bank. They said there's plenty of money in my credit card account! What is wrong with you people?"

"Please, Señor. I understand your frustration. But we ran it three times and each time, it was declined. We cannot do anything about it. You will have to make other arrangements to pay your bill."

I was scared to death. I felt like I was suffocating. At times like that, I may look angry on the outside, but the chatter in my head is far worse. I was harsh and destructive toward myself. It was a message of utter despair: *Guys like me don't succeed. Guys like me don't make it. I'm a loser. I'm a failure.*

I had only two hours before my flight departed. And the hotel was not going to let me leave without paying the bill.

Out of options, I went to a pay phone, and I called my aunt and uncle. They lived in Monterrey, Mexico.

Tia Alma answered the phone. "Juanito! ¿Como estas?"

She was happy to hear my voice because she didn't know why I was calling.

Practically in tears, I choked out, "Tia, I need your help. I'm in Guadalajara doing business meetings, but something's wrong with my credit card. It's not going through, and the hotel won't let me leave."

"Did you call your bank?"

I went through the whole story with her. After a lot of explaining, my sweet Tia Alma wired the hotel $1,000, which was a lot of money for them. I assumed it would be no problem for my boss to reimburse them instead of me.

A half hour later, the manager finally came back to me and said the wire had gone through. I was free to go. I caught a cab to the airport.

When I arrived, I sprinted in. "I have a flight that leaves in an hour," I desperately told the woman at the counter.

She looked at me like I was crazy. "Oh, you're not going to make it. See that line over there? That's immigration. You cannot leave the country without going through them first."

I went over to the immigration area. "I need to get through here. Do you have an express line or something?"

"Why are you in such a hurry to get out? What's the problem?" they asked, eying me suspiciously.

It all kept piling up. Cancelled meetings. Loneliness. Fighting with the hotel about my credit card. And now arguing with security, which is not a good place to argue.

"I have a flight that leaves in an hour."

The immigration official looked at me and said, "Sir, we're telling you right now; you're not going to make your flight."

They agreed to expedite me, but it wasn't quick enough. I ran to the gate only to find out that I missed the flight. The plane was still there—I could see it through the glass—but the last shuttle that took passengers out to the boarding area was gone.

The airline staff assured me that I could catch the next flight which was leaving in just three hours. They told me the new gate, and smiled at me as if it was good news.

By that point, I was visibly a mess. I walked to the gate for the next flight. Of course, no one was there because it wasn't going to leave for three hours. I sat there in tears. Since my credit card wasn't working, I didn't have a way to buy any food or drink. I wasn't about to drink the unfiltered water at the airport.

So I just sat. And sat. And sat.

About an hour before my flight was scheduled to leave, I looked around the gate area and noticed I was the only person there. I wondered, *Where is everybody?*

I looked up at the arrival/departure board, and I saw that the gate for my flight had changed. I hadn't heard the announcement. I found out the new gate, and ran as quickly as I could.

Sure enough, I missed the second flight.

At that point, I was furious and could barely think straight. I decided to call Becky from a payphone, which is almost impossible to do from Mexico. I had to call her collect. That was yet another infuriating experience because I had a hard time with the Mexican operator and yelled at him before I finally got through.

I told Becky what happened—just poured out my emotion. I'm so lucky to have an incredible wife. She listened, then settled me down. She has talked me down off the ledge more times than I can count.

She prayed for me and told me, "You're going to be okay." Somehow, hearing her voice and feeling her love gave me hope, and I felt calmer.

The next flight was not until the next morning at 10 a.m. I had no choice. I slept the whole night in a chair in the airport.

Chastened by all my mistakes, I must have asked a dozen people to confirm where I was supposed to be: *Which gate?*

Where is my flight? Are you sure this is the gate? Is this still the right gate? I didn't want to miss that flight! Fortunately, I did make it home that day.

In so many ways, that trip was a picture of my life at that time. It perfectly illustrates the confusion and chaos, the emotional instability, of that season.

As a postscript to the story, my boss was out of the country for a lot longer than he thought he would be. It took him a couple months—not a couple weeks—to pay me back for my expenses. My aunt and uncle were so gracious. We were finally able to pay them back but long after I'd told them we would.

There was no getting around it: the way I was working wasn't working. There was glamor and glitz when I would speak at events and talk about success principles, but behind the scenes, I wasn't succeeding like I wanted to. I knew I needed to make some changes.

 Learning Lesson Recap
We all have potential to earn money, but we also need to be smart about what is realistic. People sometimes make false promises about what they can do for us. At the time, we don't see their exaggeration—or outright deceit. Before we agree to a new job or opportunity, we must spend time doing our due diligence. In the long run, when we do the right thing, it will pay off—but usually more slowly and with less glamor than we thought.

Remember
Potential alone doesn't pay the bills!

Do not be like children in your thinking, my friends; be children so far as evil is concerned, but be grown up in your thinking.
(1 Corinthians 14:20, HCSB)

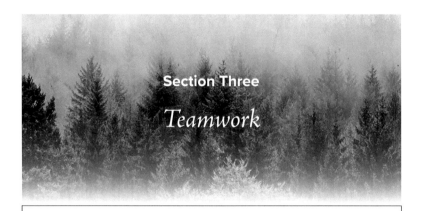

Section Three

Teamwork

Alone we can do so little; together we can do so much.

—*Helen Keller*

Talent wins games, but teamwork and intelligence
win championships.

—*Michael Jordan*

If you want to lift yourself up, lift up someone else.

—*Booker T. Washington*

Therefore encourage one another and build one another up,

just as you are doing.

—*The Apostle Paul (1 Thessalonians 5:11, ESV)*

7

A New Job

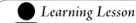

Learning Lesson
The harder you work, the luckier you get—
and every now and then, you need a little luck!

HERE'S A QUICK HISTORY LESSON, BOYS AND GIRLS: at the close of the 20th century…during the early days of the internet—before LinkedIn or online job search sites took off—if you wanted a new job, you read *newspaper want ads.*

Any of you older folks remember those?

"Juan, look at this." My wife handed me the newspaper.

I squinted at the tiny bit of newsprint copy she'd circled. The 1-inch-by-1-inch ad simply read, "Online credit card processing. Sales reps needed." The copy included a phone number.

"Don't you think that sounds interesting?" she asked.

"Yeah, I guess. What exactly is 'credit card processing'?"

"I'm not sure, but if it's part of the credit card industry and it's online, it's worth checking out."

My wife has always been a wise woman in many respects, but on that occasion—just before the start of the new millennium in the late summer of 1999—she was practically prophetic. She'd been noticing that the Internet was getting more popular. We were in the middle of the dot-com boom, and everyone was starting to talk about websites, email, and online commerce. She knew any industry that was part of that trend would be a long-term career opportunity.

I was not as aware. "I've got a bunch of other interviews this week. Do you really think I should add one more?"

Becky was unusually insistent. "Think about it, Juan. Online business is growing in leaps and bounds—it's the wave of the future. On top of that, everyone uses credit cards, and that's only going to increase. And it's a sales job—you're good at sales."

That was all true, but I still wasn't convinced.

She saw my hesitancy. "At least check it out," she added.

I thought about the other job interviews I had that week. One was with a major airline. The pay wasn't great, but I could see a future there. Besides, it would be nice to have the travel benefits. I could picture myself winging my way all around the world for almost nothing—that sounded great.

Becky's serious look, however, brought my head back down from the clouds. Becky suggested I check with a few good friends I trusted. They all agreed with Becky—that I should check out all opportunities.

So the next day I called the number on the online credit card ad and got an interview.

A few days later, I went to the airline interview. Was that a zoo! I was in a room with about 300 people. They called in each person to be interviewed. If they liked you, they'd send you to a different room. If they didn't like you, they said good-bye. I felt like we were being processed like cattle at an auction.

I made it through the first interview, and sat with the others who had passed that test. Then, they started the process again, calling us into a different room, weeding out some and sending the rest to yet another room.

I made that cut, too. By this time, it was down to about 20 people.

After about ten minutes, they called me in.

There were two interviewers behind a table. After I sat, they started right in. "Mr. Ortiz, we're curious," one of them said. "Why are you applying for a customer service job?"

"Well, frankly, I need benefits for my family. I've been doing a lot of other odd jobs these past few years, and I need something regular and consistent I can count on."

"That makes sense. But from talking to you and seeing your experience, customer service doesn't seem like the best fit. We think you'd be strong at sales. Your personality is really dynamic."

"Yeah, I am kind of wired that way," I agreed. "I mean, I've done sales. And I'm pretty good at it. But I figured I had to start somewhere with you guys, to get my foot in the door."

The other interviewer spoke. "Listen, we've got an idea. Would you be interested in sales management?"

I felt a flash of excitement, and sat up in my chair. "Tell me more."

He continued. "We feel you're more qualified to do sales management. We can put you in our training program. And within no time, we believe you could be overseeing a team of salespeople."

"That sounds great. I'd really like that."

"Great. So why don't you come back next week on Monday? We'll talk about it more and get you started."

I went home so excited. "Becky, they made me an offer—for a sales management job!" Becky was thrilled to see me so excited, and happy for the prospect of a regular paycheck coming in.

"What about the credit card processing thing? Did you follow up on that one?"

I'd actually forgotten about it.

"Well, I set up the interview for tomorrow, but now I'm not going to bother. It's in Des Plaines, and I don't really want to drive all that way for nothing. I mean, it sure seems like this airline job is a done deal, so what's the point? This is exactly what I was hoping for."

Becky wasn't buying it. "Look, you set up the interview. Why don't you just go?"

I felt a sense of frustration rising within me. "I just don't feel like it."

Becky was not one to back down—God bless her for that quality! She looked at me with that look. "I really think you should go. What have you got to lose?"

Everybody has those moments in life—those times when a decision is made, and at the time, you don't really know how important it is. Then you look back, maybe years later, and realize the whole trajectory of your life would have been different if you'd taken the other path instead of the one you decided on. This was one of those moments. My wife's wisdom and insistence on me going to that interview was one of the most pivotal crossroads of my adult life, but neither of us had any idea at the time just how significant it would be.

Here's one other thing no one could have predicted. Just a couple years later, right after the 9/11 attacks, the airline industry took a huge downward turn. Thousands of people got laid off, including many who worked for the airline that I interviewed with. I had thought it was one of most secure and growing industries in the world—and most people would have agreed with me. But it was vulnerable to the unforeseen events that changed all of our lives that September morning. Had I thrown in my lot with that company, I would likely have been just another unemployment statistic, and I would have had to start my whole job search process all over again.

So, even though I was set to start with the airline the following Monday, on Friday I went to my interview with Data Transfer Associates. The man I was supposed to meet with was Bob Hurley.

It took me over an hour to get there. It was just north of O'Hare airport, one of the busiest airports in the world, and the road traffic was just as congested as the planes in the sky. I thought, *I hate this! I would not want to make this drive every day.*

But I showed up. I rang the doorbell of the office, and the receptionist let me in and greeted me.

"Hi. Can I help you?"

"Yeah. I've got an interview with Bob Hurley."

"Oh, you do? I'm sorry, Bob isn't in the office today. Let me check with his supervisor." The receptionist told me to wait, that she'd be right back.

I thought, *You've got to be kidding! I drive all this way, and the guy isn't even here? What kind of boss sets up a job interview with a potential hire and then doesn't show?*

After a few minutes, the receptionist returned and introduced me to Kristen Gramigna, Bob's boss.

I will never forget her handshake! Strong and confident. And I could tell right away she was a sharp person. She had a great smile and welcoming personality.

After a bit of discussion trying to sort out what happened, Kristen said she'd interview me. "Thanks for coming in, Juan. Sorry for the mix-up. Come on back to my office."

As we walked through the place, I noticed the environment: it was cubicle after cubicle after cubicle. People were on phones, and it was loud. I was thinking, "Wow. This is a unique place. Lots going on here."

Once we got to Kristen's office, she started right in. We had a lively, frank conversation. I knew she was interviewing me, and she knew I was interviewing her. We were basically drilling each other in an honest, let's-see-what-you're-made-of way. I wasn't afraid to ask questions and have a little bit of an attitude. I was secure knowing I had the airline job starting Monday, so I was a little cocky. And that got Kristen's attention.

She explained the compensation structure and benefits if I took the job. Then she got a little more assertive and asked me point blank, "Do you have anything else going besides this interview?"

"Actually, yes, I have a pretty good—"

She interrupted me. "With who?"

She didn't even let me finish my sentence. But I respected her directness. She wanted to see if I was bluffing.

"Well, it's with a major corporation."

"Really? Who is it?"

"A major airline. They want me to join their management sales program."

"Really? That's great. Well, what else do you have?"

"Nothing. That's it."

"Ok, just the one. When do you start with them?"

"Actually, this coming Monday."

She sat back, looked me right in the eye and said, "Well, do me a favor. I think you need to work with us. And here's what I'd like you to do. We have a sales training program starting Monday. And Bob Hurley—who was supposed to interview you but had to go out last-minute and take care of something—he'll be doing the training for the week. We've got four new people starting. We're having huge growth. We'd love for you to be on the team."

I was surprised at her offer. "I'm flattered, but maybe you didn't hear me. I'm going to start with this other company on Monday."

"No. I heard me. That's wonderful you got that offer. But I'm giving you another one. I want you to take ours and work for us. I think once you see what's going on here and sit through a week of training, you're going to realize you did the right thing."

"I don't know…" I said. In my mind, I could see all those free airline miles blowing away in the wind.

"Let me ask you something. What do you have to lose by working for us for one week? I guarantee you with a major corporation like that, if you need to push off your start date for a week, they'll be understanding. You could go back to them if you don't like your time with us."

The words came out almost as if it was someone else talking. "Okay. I'll come back Monday."

"Terrific," she said, as if she knew all along she'd be able to persuade me. "We'll pay you for your time. And, if at the end of the week, you're not interested in staying, no problem."

She stood up and looked across the table. "So we have a deal, right?" She reached out. I stood and shook her hand.

That conversation was like an expert demonstrating what I'd always been taught about sales. You find out what the other person needs. You ask questions and listen. Once you find out what the other person is looking for, you show them how what you're offering is the very thing they want. And, when they have no other issues, you stand up, you put your hand out, and you close: *Do we have a deal?*

Kristen is an amazing salesperson, one of the best I've ever seen.

"Wonderful. Juan, I will see you Monday. I'll let Bob know you're coming."

I got in my car and thought, *What did I just do?*

When I got home, Becky asked, "So, what happened?"

I said, "Well, believe it or not, I'm going to start working there next week."

She looked a bit shocked, but then she started asking me more about the company and my impressions. "So what was it like?"

I stammered, "I can't really say."

"What do you mean?"

"I guess it's good. I was impressed with the people I met. It all happened so fast."

I explained the payment plan and the benefits. Then Becky asked, "And you took the job, right?"

"Yeah."

She looked at me for a moment with a blank, stunned stare. I didn't know if she was mad or what.

Then, ever so slowly, the faintest smile came over her face and the corners of her eyes started to twinkle. "Good," was all she said.

I went in that Monday, and I never looked back. I started that week, October of 1999.

The training was everything Kristen said it would be, and I knew I wanted to stay. The week after, I got on the floor and started making calls.

I hadn't met him personally, but I saw John Rante, the CEO and owner, walk by from time to time. We all called him "the man in the corner office" because, well, he had the corner office! One thing I noticed about John, no matter what time I got there, he was there before me; and no matter what time I left, John was still there.

I thought to myself, *This guy is relentless. He works all the time. He's the owner, but I never see him going out to play golf or whatever. He's always working.*

After I got to know John, I came to understand what I had already intuitively guessed was true. His way of thinking about his job was simple: *work harder than everyone else.* He was an incredible example to me.

Our office was one of several that Data Transfer Associates had. And ours consistently had the top sales rep every month. There were two superstars who topped the charts; and one of them, Bill Schlunz, was always number one. He is still a friend to this day.

I watched Bill and decided to make it my goal to be as good if not better than he was. I wanted to have that top sales rep honor. But it wasn't easy. The first month I almost quit because it was such a bad month. I closed only one deal my first month. I was so discouraged. I wanted instant success, and self-doubt crept in when I didn't get it.

Here's an important life lesson I learned in that period of my life. It is so easy—almost automatic—to focus on the negative. I felt like a loser because I didn't have instant success.

The irony was, I was still working my direct sales business and speaking about being positive and confident in order to achieve success. There were cassette tapes of my talks everywhere. I would walk into an airport and strangers would come up to me because they recognized me from public speaking I'd done. In certain circles, I was a famous guy. And when I was onstage, I was confident, funny, and amazing.

But when I was offstage and out of the limelight, I had trouble believing I could do sales. So after closing only one deal that first month, I needed to have a talk with Bob. "Bob, listen: I can't do this. I'm good at some sales jobs, but this one isn't working out."

Bob was very sympathetic. "Hey, it's okay. No problem. It's only your first month."

"But what am I missing? I don't understand why I'm not getting more sales."

"Tell you what, Juan. Set up some appointments, and we'll go together. You can watch me, I can watch you, and we'll see what changes might help."

I set up three appointments, and Bob went with me. I ended up just watching how he did what he did. And he closed all three! Truth is, the man was an amazing storyteller. I was impressed listening to him. Those people had no choice but to buy—it was the only way to get him out of their office! Bob and I laugh about it to this day. I saw from him that people buy because they love stories—and love those who tell them well.

Bob's style was not my style, and certainly not the only or even best way to close a deal. But I thought, if Bob Hurley can do this, I can do this.

I picked up the phone and kept at it. And to my delight, the next month I closed eight. That was the quota. Bill was closing 25 or 30. But I was pretty happy I hit quota on my second month. Third month, I got 10. Fourth month, I got 12. And then finally, my fifth month, I got 22 deals. For that month, it was enough sales for me to be the top rep.

I was so excited. I knew the next week, the first week of April, my name would be on the top sales board.

Then we found out—on the last day of March—that the office was closed. Literally, locked shut. Without any of the sales team knowing it, the company had been sold.

Then, as of April 1, we were all laid off.

Learning Lesson Recap
At times, we must make a tough choice between two really good opportunities. Set up the steps to objectively investigate each opportunity. One step should be to seek good advice from people we trust. Another is to avoid being rushed. But even when we've done all we can, there will always be a measure of uncertainty and risk. And every now and then, we just need to roll the dice and hope for the best.

Remember
The harder you work, the luckier you get—and every now and then, you need a little luck!

Remember this: Whoever sows sparingly will also reap sparingly, and whoever sows generously will also reap generously.
(2 Corinthians 9:6, NIV)

8

Rebuilding

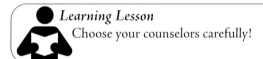

Learning Lesson
Choose your counselors carefully!

IN A MATTER OF HOURS, I watched the entire company—all my fellow employees—get laid off.

The tech support people were first. They assembled outside the conference room. One-by-one, they were called into the room, and the door closed.

It was mostly silent in the waiting area—except for a few quiet sniffles, a few hushed conversations. After a few minutes, the door would open and a now-former-employee would walk out—some were angry, some sad, some expressionless. They walked past everyone, went to their desk, and packed up their belongings. It was the same thing, person after person.

This went on all morning. After over 100 firings, my sales team finally got called in. We were the last group. The place was empty. This former buzzing hub of activity, now eerily silent. I never experienced a corporate firing before. It was surreal.

None of us knew that over a year and a half earlier, the owner, John Rante, sold his company—Data Transfer Associates, the one we worked for—to another firm called PMT. The owner of that company, Greg Daily, had now sold both companies to a huge credit card processor called Nova System. John continued working there because he was finishing out the terms of his contract with Greg.

John Rante introduced me to Greg, and I later worked with him also. Over the years, I got to know Greg well. Through industry events, as friends, and mostly playing golf, I really enjoy being around Greg. He is positive, encouraging, fun—and also competitive. Even though he's successful, he's very down-to-earth and cares about people. He's become a good friend I trust.

The main reason Nova System bought our company was for our customers—all the merchants. They didn't need any of our staff. So with the deal now complete, all of us were out.

Not everybody was sad. We all got a severance check for $1,000–$2,000, and for those who were thinking of leaving anyway, this was a nice parting gift. I'd been there six months,

Greg Daily and John Rante

and getting any severance after working less than a year seemed like a sweet deal. I was still speaking at direct sales events, so I wasn't as worried about making the transition. I was sure I could find another job fairly quickly. After all, I'd been bouncing from job to job for a few years before this, so to me it didn't feel that tragic. I felt like I was going to be OK.

After all of us on the sales team got our severance agreements and signed the necessary legal documents, one of the Nova System guys came out to address us all at once.

"Before you go, we wanted to tell you that Nova is going to keep this building open for about another 30 to 60 days. Any of you who want to continue selling with us, you can. It'll be straight commission—there will be no base salary or benefits. You'll be paid for each new customer."

I thought about it and decided, *Why not?* About ten of us (out of the 30 who had been there) stayed on. I closed 22 deals that month, and I knew I was getting a good commission check. I was confident I could keep that up for as long as they let me work there.

Of the ten sales team members that stayed on, only six of us were there after the first week. And now, every lead that came in off the fax machine was shared between six guys instead of 25. It was like fishing with dynamite—the nets were suddenly overflowing. That month, I closed 40 deals. Because the staff was so small, we couldn't help but succeed.

I told Becky, "This is fantastic. I've never done so well at a job." And, because we were straight commission, we could set our own hours. I could work from home or drive to the office after the morning rush hour was over. It was a good deal on all fronts.

After about a month, I got a call from my former sales manager, Bob Hurley.

"Hey, what are you up to?" he asked.

"I'm still here working for Nova."

"You're kidding!"

"No. They offered to let us stay for a while."

Bob was amazed. "Well, that's great. Who else is there?"

I listed off my co-workers, all of whom used to work for Bob. "It's straight commission—no benefits or anything—but the few of us left here are killing it."

"Very cool, Juan, I'm happy for you."

"Thanks. So, what are *you* up to?"

"Funny you should ask. We've started a new company called Online Data. John, Kristen, Bill, myself, and a few other people have been at this since we all left DTA. I'm calling because we'd like you to come work with us."

As we talked more, I found out that the day after everybody left Data Transfer Associates, John and the others moved into a rented office space to build a new company, Online Data Corp. It was about 30 minutes closer to my house. Though the new venture was John's idea, and he was the CEO, he wanted everyone who helped him get it off the ground to be part owner.

I also found out how forward-looking John was. Back in the early '80s, he registered the name "Online Data Corp." He was certain the online business model was going to be big. He believed it was prudent to have one or two S-corporations formed and ready to go, so when he got a good idea, he could build it quickly into a viable enterprise. So he created this company called Online Data Corp, which up until 1999 hadn't been anything except a name on paper. The time was right for a new business initiative, and he had the legal structure in place to bring it to life.

"Wow, Bob. That sounds really interesting. And Westchester is closer to my house. But, here's the thing: I really, *really* need benefits. Even though I don't have any now, my situation is temporary. My wife would never let me commit to anything long-term without having benefits guaranteed."

Truthfully, Becky wasn't the only one who wanted that additional security. By then, we had five kids, and we needed to have insurance.

Bob thought for a minute. "Well, we don't have enough working capital to pay you a salary just yet—you'll be on commission for the near term. But I think we could include some benefits. Then later, I believe we'll be in a place to also pay you a salary."

"That sounds like a pretty good deal. I do have one more concern, though. What about paid leave?"

"Sure. We'll give you some vacation time as well."

"Let me talk it over with Becky and get back to you. I can tell you right now, though, I think she'll go for it."

Becky was delighted with the offer. So I gave my notice at Nova and joined Online Data.

It was like we got the band back together! John was the CEO, Kristen the VP of sales, and Bob the sales manager—with me as "up-front vocals": the lead salesman.

I remember the contrast on my first day walking into their tiny office. I mean, it was a no-frills environment—definitely looked like a start-up.

"Welcome back, Juan," John said. "Nice to see you again. Hope you're ready to roll up your sleeves."

Both Data Transfer Associates and this new company, Online Data Corp, were what the industry refers to as an ISO, an Independent Sales Organization. An ISO registers with a sponsoring bank like Wells Fargo. Then they start building an account portfolio. We were selling to various businesses the ability to accept credit cards and process payments.

In his previous company, John built a portfolio of businesses that used our processing, and then sold it for a nice profit. But when a company like that sells, the buyers don't need the people who service those accounts. They want the big accounts and roll those into their current serving systems. Nova liked the portfolio with all these loyal customers and bought that.

John realized he could do that all over again—build another portfolio, then sell it in a few years. So, without delay, he started this new company. Only now I was getting in on the ground floor. And among other benefits, I got stock options.

I started in May, and things were going well. Yet lurking in the background was another company that started wooing me away from John's new venture. These people I had known for years were also in the credit card processing industry. Excited about the possibility of working with friends I'd known for a long time, I actually decided to leave Online Data Corp shortly after I joined. I told John what I was planning to do. He was not happy.

"Look, Juan. The company you're looking at is not good. I know them well. I encourage you not to go."

Even Bob Hurley said, "Don't do this, Juan. John is the right man to be with. You will regret it if you leave."

Yet my good friend kept at me. "Come work with us. It's going to be great." The picture he painted looked too good to pass up.

Like so many people, I went for the shiny thing. When we're hypnotized by dazzling promises and then others point out conflicting evidence, we reason it away. We decide with our emotions and turn away from facts we'd rather not deal with.

John had a warning before I left. "Look, Juan. I have a policy that when someone leaves my company, they're never hired again. I don't let people come back when they quit on me."

"I understand the consequences, and I respect your position. It's not personal at all, John. It just feels like this is a better opportunity."

John couldn't get excited for me. "You have to do what you think is best for you and your family, but I'm going to ask you one final time not to quit. It's not just about our loss, it's about what I think is going to happen to you. There is more to them than meets the eye, and it is not a good situation you're walking into."

In the course of our decision-making, Becky was having doubts. As much as I saw potential in this new company, even I wasn't 100 percent sure it was the right move. I liked John and saw his high morals and proven track record. A future with him would be good. But my friend's enthusiasm and insistence wore down my resistance and persuaded me to go with the other company.

As soon as I started there, I was successful. I had a great first month, an even stronger second month. My apprehension faded as I saw I could do as well there as I'd done in my former company.

But then customers started calling. They were angry and said, "Hey, we still haven't received our credit card machine" or "When are we going to get our funds?"

Worse than the complaints was watching how the owners dealt with them. They did nothing. I could sell, but what was the point if our products and service were lousy? It was only a matter of time before my credibility as a salesman—and as a Christian man of integrity—came into question.

By November, I started to buckle under the pressure. Watching the owners' behavior was maddening. Unlike John, who was there every day before any employee got there and was the last one to leave, these guys were rarely in the office. They'd roll in about 10 a.m., take two-hour lunches, and leave early. Long weekends that gobbled up Fridays and Mondays were the norm. The work ethic there was appalling. I hated it.

By the middle of December, I told Becky I was unhappy and wanted to quit. Customers yelled at me on the phone because I sold them something that never got delivered or properly supported. So a week before Christmas, I resigned.

In the back of my mind, I thought, *I'm doing lots of speaking in the direct sales business, and there's some money coming in from that. Things are great with my marriage and my kids. I don't have all this pressure on me like other guys. I'll chill for a few weeks and find another job after the new year.*

Then, in early January, I got a call that changed everything.

 Learning Lesson Recap
Life is full of twists and turns. Be careful not to be dazzled or hypnotized by a flashy road sign. Not all counsel—or counselors—are equal. Trust the guidance only from those worthy of trust.

 Remember
Choose your counselors carefully!

The way of a fool is right in his own eyes, but a wise man listens to advice.

(Proverbs 12:15, ESV)

9

A Second Chance

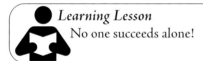

Learning Lesson
No one succeeds alone!

"Hey Juan, how's it going?" It was Bob Hurley, my former boss.

"I'm pretty good. How are you? How was Christmas?"

"Great. We're all doing great. I was wondering how the new job is working out?"

I didn't feel any need to sugar-coat it. "Truthfully? Not so good, Bob. In fact, I quit last month."

He was silent for a minute. "I'm sorry to hear that."

"You were right, Bob. John was right. You tried to warn me not to go there. I wouldn't listen. But once I saw how they operated, I couldn't in good conscience stay. And I wouldn't blame you if you said, 'I told you so.'"

"Juan, that's not at all what I'm feeling. I was hoping it would work out. In fact, because you were there, I referred some people to you guys."

"You're being way too gracious. I blew it. I was blind, and I know that now."

"Look, I didn't call to make you feel bad, Juan. This changes the whole purpose of my call. I wanted to see how you were doing. But now that I know things didn't work out for you there, what would you think of coming back?"

"*Coming back?* To work for you and John?"

"Yeah. You haven't been gone that long. We could get you up to speed in no time."

"I don't know, Bob. I've got several speaking engagements lined up and I was thinking of just doing that for a while and see if I can build that up."

Then I admitted what was going on under the surface. "Here's what's most painful. I really let you guys down. I'm embarrassed by my foolishness."

"Everybody makes mistakes, Juan. You get to make a few, too."

"Kind of you to say that. But I don't understand. Even if I agree to consider your offer, John was very clear. Once you leave, you can't be re-hired. Right? How can you promise me a second chance if that's his rule?"

"I think I can make the case for you as an exception. We know how hard you work, what you can do, and we know what kind of a person you are. One lapse of judgment shouldn't be the only factor determining your future."

Later that afternoon, the phone rang. It was Bob.

"Juan, I have good news! I talked to John, and he's willing to set aside his rule this time. If you're really serious, he's willing to give you another chance. But he's not going to do it unless you're committed to staying and working hard. If that doesn't happen, you'll be out."

I knew right away I should take him up on this incredibly gracious offer. So I said yes.

My first day, I was impressed with all the changes. I'd been gone for about four months. In that time, those guys had tripled the size of the business. There were 20 people working there, and the office had doubled in size. It was incredible.

The new job was straight commission with insurance and vacation time. I had a tiny cubicle and a phone. But because I was straight commission, I didn't have to keep regular hours or sit in that cubicle all day. I could use my time however I thought best. I was good at being productive, visiting potential clients, making calls from home, taking trips to the office when it was convenient for me (and there wasn't traffic to waste my time).

Like before, it all came naturally. I signed up restaurants and other businesses faster than anybody else. I built a network of referrals. People called me and said, "Hey, you're the credit card guy, right? Can you set up our store? We're opening a new location." Business was great.

On a typical day, I made some calls, drove to a customer's store, set up the machine, did the paperwork, made a few more calls, saw another customer or two, and then at the end of the day, I dropped off the paperwork at the office and said hi to everybody.

One day, in the spring of 2001, John asked to talk to me.

"Juan, we're launching a new online application product. We're going to some trade shows to get the word out. I'd like you to come along to represent us. Any leads we get there will be yours to close, plus I'll pay you for your time each day."

"I think that would be great!"

"We need someone dynamic like you to make lots of contacts, shake a lot of hands and explain our application in an interesting and compelling way. The first show is here in Chicago, so there won't be any travel for this one."

After three weeks of preparation and learning the new product, we went to the trade show. I was totally in my element. It was a blast.

Tradeshow Team

John liked my personality—how outgoing and funny I was. But these guys knew me only as a salesman in professional settings. They didn't have a clue about how well-known I was as a public speaker in direct sales circles.

There we were on the exhibit floor of a big hotel in Chicago. Donned in matching golf shirts sporting our logo, we stood in a 10′x10′ booth with our brochures and business cards. People walked through the aisles. Because I'm a people person, my job was to stand out in the aisle shaking people's hands.

Random people walked up and said, "Hey, Juan!" with an expression of familiarity. A lot of times, I couldn't place the person, so I just responded in kind, "Hey, how are you doing?" While my team looked at me, the guy said, "I'm a friend of Juan's." Two minutes passed, and it happened again. And then again. Before long, 20 people had greeted me by name.

John was baffled. People explained they knew me from hearing me speak at a conference or business meeting. Direct sales made me quite popular.

A few times, someone got emotional and teared up. They hugged me and asked one of the team standing nearby, "Hey, would you take a picture of Juan and me together?"

John was blown away. He dug deeper as more and more people came up.

"Let me understand. You heard Juan speak, right?"

"Oh, yeah. Several times. As a matter of fact, I have three of his tapes."

"You have *tapes* of him?"

"Oh my goodness, yes. You should hear his talk, "Don't Mess With Me." It's the best! Juan talks about how he's a Mexican with money now. *Don't even mess with me!*"

For the next two days, random people stopped by our booth to see me. When word got out I was there, it was crazy. A ton of direct sales people stopped by, wanting my autograph.

They also asked me, "What are you doing here? Why are you working this booth?" They didn't understand why a big-time direct sales personality was at a trade show that had nothing to do with that business.

I didn't hesitate to tell them the truth. "I work with this company."

They were confused. If I was a successful direct sales guy, why was I working a normal job? "Wait, you have to work? I thought you were financially free and independent."

I explained that working with this firm was a good opportunity and provided benefits for me, my wife and five kids. I never said in any of my talks that I didn't have other work besides direct sales. But most people assumed anybody speaking as frequently as I did must have been at the top and didn't need to work any more. Truthfully, it felt awkward at first. But I think the main thing prompting their questions was that they were curious about my life.

Everybody on my team was blown away by my popularity at the trade show. John invited me to go to trade shows in Los

Angeles, Atlanta, and New York. For the next two years, we traveled to about five trade shows a year. And every place we went, people knew me.

It wasn't that surprising to me. Over the years I had spoken on stages to tens of thousands of people. I had four or five tapes that were sold all over the country and were listened to by a couple million people.

I was an inspiration to others. They'd come up to me and say, "You're Juan Ortiz" like someone saying, "You're Elvis Presley." And they often quoted my talk where I said, "Don't mess with me!" I'd say, "Yeah, that's me." At every trade show, I got hugged and photographed.

I was treated like a celebrity because, in those circles, I was one. At the height of my involvement in that business, I arrived at a speaking engagement in a limo that had been sent for me. I went backstage where there were refreshments and first-class accommodations. I came out on stage to thunderous applause and spoke to 5,000 people at a time. When I was done, I got a standing ovation. Afterward, people stood in line to talk to me or get an autograph.

But with John and the team, I was in a different world, the world of sales and credit card processing. Yet when people recognized me in that booth, it was as if I had just finished one of my talks and they were coming for autographs. My colleagues watched in disbelief.

My favorite story of celebrity status happened when John and I were in Las Vegas. Before dinner, he wanted to go bet on some Blackhawk games, because he loved hockey. We made the bets, then went to dinner. After dinner, we went back to the sportsbook to find out who won and who lost.

The sportsbook was closed. The restaurant was closed. Even the bar was closed. But the big boards were up and running. We checked our ticket, reading the results on these huge lit up panels. John and I were looking up at the screen, and all of a sudden I heard an Australian accent say, "Juan Ortiz! Hey mate, is that you?"

Imagine how this looked to John. We're in Vegas, at the Bellagio at 11:00 at night, and this guy from the other side of the world walks up to greet me! What's more, I recognized him immediately. He was a very successful direct sales guy from Australia who had invited me over there to speak. He and his wife were with a group of 20 people who had won a trip from Australia to Las Vegas for their sales rewards. They were out having coffee late at night.

This guy happened to be walking back and saw me. He sounded like an ad for Outback Steakhouse with his Aussie accent. I responded right away, greeting him by name. We hugged, and then he called his friends over and started introducing me to all of them.

John looked at me with absolute amazement. His arms were crossed. He looked at my Aussie friend and finally spoke.

"You know Juan, and you're from *Australia?*"

My friend nodded. "Juan is the greatest speaker you will ever find."

Then the whole group was hugging me, talking to me, and taking pictures.

For all the times that sort of recognition happened, even for me that was one of the weirdest chance meetings. But John still talks about it to this day. What are the odds that we'd run into people from Australia in Vegas? And that they'd recognize me? And that they would be ecstatic because, in their eyes, I was a superstar?

Over the years, I was as faithful as I knew how to be with the opportunities that came along. Whether it was the direct sales business or youth work or selling credit card processing, I never knew how any of it would pay off. But I kept putting one foot in front of the other. I kept challenging myself to do better. When I felt like quitting, I let other people encourage me. I knew I couldn't make it alone, so I sought mentors. I took correction when I needed it and tried not to be defensive.

I say this not because I did it all perfectly. But I never gave up trying. I was willing to change.

Believe me, I made plenty of mistakes. I crossed ethical lines and had to face the consequences. In fact, I was about to find out just how slippery I could be. Envelopes stuffed with $100 bills would present a new test. If you've ever struggled to stay honest and accountable with money, maybe you'll see yourself in what happened next.

 Learning Lesson Recap
We all have gifts, talents, and abilities that can help us succeed to the highest levels. But rarely can we make it to the top without help. For the few who go it alone, they don't hang onto their gains for very long. True success comes from building a community, a team of people around us—who believe in us, challenge us and work side-by-side with us. Those are the people who will celebrate success—and all of life—with us, too!

Remember
No one succeeds alone!

Two are better than one, because they have a good return for their labor: if either of them falls down, one can help the other up. But pity anyone who falls and has no one to help them up.... Though one may be overpowered, two can defend themselves. And a cord of three strands is not quickly broken.

(Ecclesiastes 4:9–12, NIV)

10

Learning the Business

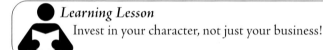

Learning Lesson
Invest in your character, not just your business!

WE SAT IN A CONFERENCE ROOM, having one last meeting with our sales management team before heading to the airport. As the meeting closed, my boss John handed me an envelope. I looked inside. There were several hundred-dollar bills inside.

"This is petty cash for miscellaneous expenses," he said. "Use it during the trip to buy lunch, dinner, a cab ride, whatever you need." John knew I didn't have spending cash, so I believe he provided it for me to use on this and future trips. He was right—I was really broke, and needed it.

Several hundred dollars for a trip was a lot of money for me. I decided I would spend as little as possible and keep the rest.

Trips like this started happening more and more. Most trips, I'd get more cash to spend. Using my frugal ways, I found ways to hang on to almost half of it.

I knew the excess cash wasn't meant to end up in my wallet. But I figured this was my spending money and I could do whatever I wanted with it. Nobody ever asked me about it, and it certainly didn't create any significant downturn in the company's profitability.

Yet that's not how integrity works. A misdeed is still unethical, even if you can get away with it. Taking something that isn't yours is wrong, even if the one you stole from can afford the loss. But my self-centered rationalization allowed me to pocket that money with hardly a pang of guilt. Truth is, there are times when a calloused conscience doesn't speak loud enough to guide a person well, and I was definitely not paying attention to the whispers of my internal moral compass. I'm ashamed of it now, but that's how dysfunctional I was back then.

John was so patient with me. Though we never talked about it directly, I think he suspected I didn't use all the cash for my trips. I was slow to face the fact that this was not my money. Those dollars were company assets that I was supposed to use for the trips' expenses.

It's like there were two people in me—the Juan who did what was right, and the Juan who tried to get away with whatever he could. Every now and then, those two faced off and argued. But mostly, I compartmentalized my life; I let each lead me whenever it seemed best to put that Juan in charge. So, although I had heard the instructions to get receipts and then return the unused money, I just never did that. And for some reason, our accountant never asked about it, either.

I now call my actions what they were: *stealing.* But as I said before, back then, I foolishly thought, "The company just gave me 500 bucks. Whether I use it for a client's needs or mine, we're both important people who keep this business running!"

I even went so far as to think, *If John was willing to throw around money like that, why should I worry about it? It's just petty change no one cares about.*

Ironically, John's consistent example of integrity was one of the influences that caused me to reconsider what I was doing. That, and my Christian convictions, which had never left me—though I had stifled their influence. John's honorable way of dealing with clients and employees convicted me. He didn't just talk about the value of ethical behavior, he gave me a concrete, living example to imitate. It became almost irresistible to want to be like him.

That leads me to a very important observation about my life. When I think of what a terrible legacy my dad left me, it's not all that surprising that I had so much to learn about adult life. Even though I'd taught myself how to survive as a boy, the real secret to the big changes I've made in my character has been the influence of several key mentors. I know that I must give all the credit to God for his amazing patience and love for me; yet when I think of how God actually helped me, in day-to-day living, the main tool in his hands was patient and loving people.

Wanting to be good in the abstract didn't motivate or change me, but *good people,* showing up and giving me examples to follow, did.

John was just such a key mentor. His example of integrity helped me see my own lack of it. Just watching him in action taught me so much. But beyond that, he consistently pulled me aside to teach me about good business practices. He played an active role in shaping me.

I'll never forget an early meeting he had with me. "Juan," he said, "one of the keys to getting ahead in business is to tap into the experience of others. Don't be intimidated by people who know more than you—seek them out and learn from them."

That concept wasn't all that surprising—I was constantly asking for John's input as we worked together. But he added something else that stuck with me. "When you ask someone for advice or help, offer them something in return. Don't just be a taker. You don't have to pay them a consultant fee; but if you invite them to lunch, pick up the tab. If you meet them in their office, bring a simple gift to show your appreciation. You're not 'buying' their advice; but you are showing respect—you're valuing their time. Don't ever sit across the table at lunch with a successful person who's giving you an hour or so to share wisdom or answer questions at your request and not at least pay for the meal."

I squirmed. Many times I had done that very thing: I would ask John to lunch, pepper him with questions, and then nonchalantly sit back and wait for him to pick up the check!

I had a bunch of dumb reasons for my lack of generosity. I mean, let's start with the obvious: he's the CEO of a multi-million dollar company. He makes a lot more money than I do. Plus, if I become a better employee as a result of these meetings with him, I'll make more money for the company. And that will surely enrich him eventually, right? So it's perfectly reasonable to expect him to pay for the meal!

It's just that I wasn't showing respect.

What would you do? There was a time I didn't even give it a second thought. Now I see all those excuses—*This person is rich, They have so much money, I'm practically broke*—just don't cut it. That is not the way to success. If you have the opportunity to sit in front of a multi-millionaire or anyone else you think can show you the way to a better life—even if you talk for only an hour—you should be willing to pick up a lunch tab. It doesn't matter if that person can afford it more easily than you.

True to his nature, John was gracious toward me as I started to be more mindful of this principle—just like he was with so many other lessons I learned from him. Some of those took longer to turn into habits than others. But to this day, whenever I am sitting at the table across from a successful man or woman, I do not expect that person to pay anything when they help me. I will insist on taking care of the meal.

Wisdom and understanding are valued by God. The Bible says, "Blessed are those who find wisdom, those who gain understanding; it is more profitable than silver and yields better returns than gold" (Proverbs 3:13–14, NIV).

Wisdom is worth paying for.

Very few people understand the value of wisdom. I make it no secret that I have found so much of that wisdom in the teachings of the Bible. I really do treat reading and studying that book like I'm digging for silver or gold.

You can also get wisdom by listening to wise people. But you have to be teachable. If you're surrounded by wise people, but you shut them out, you won't get the value. I am so very glad for the accumulated wisdom that I have received in my life from God's Word and good people.

As I progressed in the company, John put me in a unique position to help lead others while I continued developing my own leadership skills. And I'm very thankful. He was there to correct me when I made mistakes. He was there to catch me when I fell. He was also there to high-five me and clap for me and praise me and award me when I did great things.

It wasn't always easy. I sometimes led people who criticized me. I led people who eventually quit and then blamed me for stuff. There were people who hated me and wanted to switch departments to get away from me. That was hard. Dealing with rejection as a leader is always painful—especially when I was sure I had their best interest in mind, but they misunderstood. I used to think if you did the right thing, people would appreciate you. But that's naive. And when those people criticized me, or unjustly accused me, John continued to believe in me. His support helped me to move forward with confidence.

❖

I want to share one more story about John's influence on me before closing this chapter.

I did a lot of speaking in my industry. I remember one speaking gig in particular that led to an opportunity for me to learn and for our company to grow.

I sat in the back of a crowded auditorium, next to my friend. He was just about to give his talk, and then I was going to be the last speaker.

"How's business?" I asked, just making conversation.

"Good," he said. "It's going good, but I'm kind of looking for a new thing."

I sensed he seemed uncomfortable with what he just shared.

He quickly changed the subject. "So what are you guys working on these days?"

"Business is good. We're expanding," I said.

"How's John doing?" he asked.

"He's great. I really enjoy working with him. He really teaches me a lot."

Just then, he was called to the podium. We parted, and I didn't give the exchange another thought. Fast forward about a month. My phone rings.

"Hey Juan." It was my boss, John.

"Oh, hello, John," I answered. "I'm surprised to hear from you. I thought you were on vacation."

"Well, yes, I am. But you'll never guess what happened," he said.

"Okay, what?" I asked.

"Your friend called me," he said, referring to the man I had chatted with at the speaking engagement.

"Huh, what a coincidence. I just saw him about a month ago. What did he call you for?"

"He wants to sell his company."

"Hmm. He was asking me all kinds of questions about what we're up to, how we're doing. Now that conversation makes sense."

"Look, I'm gonna sit down and talk to him when I get back from vacation. But in the meantime," he instructed, "I want you to do some research on his company."

John was training me to evaluate business opportunities. It was a good thing I did, too, because this man's company was in trouble. They really needed to sell.

When John got back, he looked over my input and did a little asking around of his own. Then he met with this friend of mine and his CFO and a couple of the other leaders at our office. Based on the research we both had done, John made an offer. But the amount he was willing to spend was almost an insult to my friend. It wasn't even close—not even half of what they were hoping for. Unfortunately, based on our evaluation of the company, it was clear that they were not worth the price they were asking. This guy was really in trouble.

We parted ways without a deal.

Just days after our conversation, the bank called the note. And then it got even worse. Without any indications of what he was about to do, my friend took his own life. We were all shocked to hear of it.

A few weeks later, the CFO called us again. "John, you're the only person who gave us a legitimate offer. We've lost a lot of employees. The place is in shambles. But we have a very nice portfolio. Would you reconsider?"

John told me about the CFO's renewed negotiation attempt and invited me to come with him to evaluate what was going on.

This time, we met in their offices. Just walking in, we tried not to show our shock. The paint on the walls was chipping. A few employees sat at their desks, on chairs that were ripped. They did not look happy.

After looking around for a while, John took me aside. "Juan, why don't you spend some time here? Spend a month with this sales team, and tell me what you think."

As messy and chaotic as that office was, I knew this was an opportunity to learn and to be part of an important decision. So I spent a month there, trying to find the strengths and the weaknesses of their system.

I could see that it was a really horrible place to work. But I was trying to evaluate objectively. Did they actually have a good portfolio of business that could be a basis for future growth? Was it just mismanagement that led to their current troubles, or was their whole business model flawed?

Even the best captain with a great crew can't keep a sinking ship afloat. I needed to know if there was anything there that could be salvaged, or if things were just too far gone.

After my time there, John asked, "What are you thinking?"

"We need to let a bunch of people go. A lot of people didn't like the sales manager, but I felt he was really good at training and selling. I think they've got a good system. And with the right support team behind him, I think this could be a profitable acquisition."

When it comes to business, John makes his own decisions. Even though I was the guy actually going to this office, spending time with these people, getting to know them, the decision was John's based on what he saw as well as what I told him. John could have done all that on his own, but being a good mentor, he involved me so I could learn.

We bought the company.

Then John really surprised me. "Juan, I want you to oversee operations."

For the next three years, I went down to the new firm's office a couple of times a week and oversaw the whole thing. We got rid of people. We hired some new talent. Today, that office is huge. It's in a much more beautiful location, and people like working there. The team is trained and effective, and the leadership is flourishing, doing what they are good at. Really, it's a whole new ballgame. I'm proud of what we accomplished.

Six months after buying that company, I wanted to get some feedback. I called John. "Can we evaluate how I'm doing with getting this company turned around?"

"Absolutely. Why don't we have dinner together? I can drive down to the city and meet you. I could do the 28th or the 29th."

I looked at my calendar and realized he was scheduling our dinner three weeks out. That seemed like a long time to wait. When I asked to meet, I meant later this week, not later this month. I felt a bit frustrated. Was I not a priority?

My old insecurities rose up. *Maybe he's really unhappy. Maybe I made a huge mistake here, and he's putting off having to tell me the bad news. Maybe he's going to fire me!*

The next three weeks, I was so up and down. By the time we got to that dinner, I wasn't sure if I'd be able to even eat.

We sat in a booth at the steakhouse, and I looked down at the white tablecloth, uncertain.

John spoke first. "Juan, I know I put you off for these three weeks," he began. "But I wanted to really spend some time thinking about this. I wanted to do the best thing I could to help you—to help you understand the big picture of the past six months."

He pulled out a sheet of paper and slid it across the table to me. It was a bulleted list, with ten points. I was shocked to read that each of those points was something I was doing right! John understood the power of building someone up, and doing so with very specific feedback. He had taken the time to think about and write out each point. That's how he started the evaluation.

First and foremost, he wanted to make sure I knew he valued me. He told me how important I was. The relief I felt quickly turned into amazement.

"You are really good at this, Juan. I love how you've managed the new company. You're gifted. I don't think there's anyone else in our company who could have done this job. This is just one more shining example of how you bring so much value to the team."

I was nearly in tears; it was overwhelming.

Then, because he's a good leader, he also offered some ways I could be even better. "The way I see it, there are only a few things I think would improve how you're managing this." And he gave me those two or three points. Then, he concluded on a positive note. "Outside of those two or three little things, Juan, what a great job you're doing! We are very fortunate to have you as a leader in our organization."

I was so moved, but I controlled my emotions as we ate. We finished dinner, and I walked to the station to catch a train home. Sitting on the train, I fought back tears. What just happened? Here is this man I respect, and he's building me up that much. It was incredible.

Just the opposite of my dad, who berated me, belittled me, called me names. He treated my mom like dirt and my siblings like they were cockroaches. He tried to rip off people in business, and he thought everybody was stupid and not worth his time. Growing up, that was my example for how adult men treated people.

John showed me something so different. He was super successful. He got it and wanted me to get it. The first four or five years working with John, I didn't realize what a privilege it was. What a blessing to know a man like that, the CEO of my company, willing to mentor and teach me and make himself available to me. He invited me to learn about business and had enough personal security to let me try things and learn by doing.

God has blessed me with a lot of people who have come alongside me, mentoring and helping me. But in a business environment, I never experienced anyone like John Rante. I owe so much to him.

 Learning Lesson Recap
So many people fail at business (and life!) not because of lack of knowledge but because of lack of character. We need to find role models of good character as well as good business. Then we must make the investment of time and money to meet with those people so they can teach us what they know.

Remember
Invest in your character, not just your business!

Blessed are those who find wisdom, those who gain understanding; it is more profitable than silver and yields better returns than gold.

(Proverbs 3:13–14, NIV)

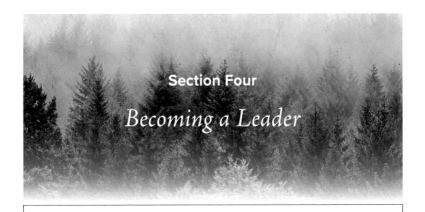

Becoming a Leader

It's not about money or connections –
it's the willingness to outwork and outlearn everyone.

—*Mark Cuban*

Management is doing things right;
leadership is doing the right things.

—*Peter F. Drucker*

There are no secrets to success.

It is the result of preparation, hard work,
and learning from failure.

—*Colin Powell*

Work hard and become a leader; be lazy and become a slave.

—*Proverbs 12:24, NLT*

11

Cars

Learning Lesson
Hard work is fueled by desire for a better life!

I TIPTOED INTO THE OFFICE, trying to look inconspicuous. I was late for work—again.

I approached my boss Bob Hurley's open office door. I figured I could walk by quickly to get to my office and not be seen. But he was sitting at his desk facing the door. I made a dash for it.

"Juan!" he called out.

Busted. I backed up. "Hey, Bob. How's it going?" I matter-of-factly replied.

"You're late! You have got to get here on time," Bob continued.

When I first started working at Data Transfer, I reported to Bob Hurley. I was supposed to get to the office at 8 a.m. With Chicago traffic, it typically took me almost an hour to get there.

If everything went well. Which it often didn't.

"Sorry, Bob. I had a little car trouble…again," I said sheepishly.

Bob just rolled his eyes. This was getting to be a pattern.

A little car trouble was putting it mildly. At the time, I drove an old beater, a 1989 Cadillac Deville. It was a long, black, four-door sedan. In its day, it was probably somebody's pride and joy. But it was at least ten years old when I got it. On the outside, it retained a shadow of its luxury appearance. But inside, it was a wreck. The felt liner on the ceiling was coming loose and strips of it hung down. The fraying threads sometimes brushed against me and felt like a spider crawling on my neck. The seats were ripped. The air conditioning didn't work, and most of the time, neither did the heat. The thing guzzled gas—so a huge part of my commission checks each month wafted out the tailpipe as exhaust fumes.

The real problem was the engine. It would die on me all the time. I would literally have to coast to a stop, wait five minutes while it did whatever cars do when they're given a "time out" for bad behavior, and then start it up again. The wasted time and the embarrassment of it all was ridiculous. But I just didn't have the money to fix it. So whenever I drove to work (or went anywhere), if it died on the road, I'd pull over, wait, and then start it up, hoping I'd make it the rest of the way before it acted up.

Old beater cars were something I was very familiar with. Growing up, my dad always had junked cars in our yard. Some worked, some didn't. My brothers and I would play on them, as sort of a poor-kid's jungle-gym. Unfortunately, they were dangerous—with torn, rusty bits sticking out just waiting to dig into a little boy's skin. Of the cars that did run, we never had a decent one to use. My dad was the only one with a license, and, though he would sometimes drive us around, we didn't like to be with him if we could avoid it. So, as often as

My Old Cadillac, "Black Beauty"

we could, my siblings and I would bum rides, or take the bus, or just walk whenever we had to get somewhere.

Now I was driving "Black Beauty" as we called her. I tried to keep my sense of humor about my predicament. I'd pretend I was some cool dude, driving a low-rider, turning heads and being the envy of all who saw me. I knew I wasn't, but it was fun to pretend. At work, I'd get teased about my ride, but it was actually kind of cool knowing I had this trademark set of wheels and was infamous for it.

Most days at lunch, I offered to drive my sales team to a nearby restaurant. The guys knew Black Beauty might not start. They knew we might not get back on time. But they were willing to go on an adventure with me.

When my boss overheard us making plans, he would say, "Take somebody else's car, okay? I can't have six of my sales reps out for lunch and not be able to make it back on time."

Eventually Black Beauty bit the dust. Simply died. I sold it to a junkyard for $50. I replaced it with another huge Cadillac—this one was white.

Bob decided the car's name should be "White Lightning," though it was anything but fast!

White Lightning was a bit nicer than Black Beauty. The upholstery was intact. It had air conditioning that still worked. But I couldn't seem to shake off the curse of an unreliable engine. Both of my cars had almost the same problem—the engine would literally cut out, and I would coast off the road and have to wait for about ten minutes, then start it up again. The difference was that White Lightning also belched smoke from under the hood just before it died. So now I also had to wait for the smoke to clear before I could start her up again.

One time, soon after I started driving White Lightning, I went to a trade show at McCormick Place, a convention center in Chicago, just south of downtown. Patrice from HR walked up to me as we were ending our day at the booth.

"Hey, Juan. Do you think Kim and I could get a ride home from you on Thursday night?" Kim was one of my sales reps, and she'd been working at the booth as well.

"Sure, no problem," I told her. "I've got a big car, plenty of room."

Patrice and Kim worked with me but didn't know about White Lightning yet.

So that Thursday, at the end of the day, we headed out to the parking lot. The drive from that part of the city out to the suburb where our office was would take more than an hour in rush hour traffic.

We got to the car, and I unlocked the doors.

"Wow, this is nice." Patrice said.

"It's a Cadillac DeVille," I said nonchalantly. "I call her *White Lightning.*"

We all piled in. With its spacious interior, the back seat of that thing felt like a limousine.

"This is huge! The interior is so big." I could tell they were impressed.

I started her up (she was always reliable at the beginning of the ride), and we headed out. We merged onto the Stevenson Expressway, where traffic was crawling, bumper to bumper. Even though it was early evening on a summer day, it was still 90 degrees out. As we drove slowly out of the city, I thought, "Oh, please, God. This is not going to be good." I knew the weather and crawling along that slow would do a number on poor White Lightning.

Right around the Cicero Avenue exit, a little smoke started coming up from the front of the car.

"Um, hey, Juan?" said Kim. "There's smoke coming from your hood."

Patrice looked worried, too. "Oh, my goodness. Is everything okay?"

"Don't worry, ladies. Happens all the time. It'll be fine, trust me," I lied.

Just then, a convertible pulled up beside me. A very attractive blonde looked over at me from the driver's side. Out of the corner of my eye, I could tell she was totally checking me out. I glanced over and could now see she was definitely looking right at me. I winked, draping my hand over the steering wheel, nodding at her with the coolest, dapper smile I had.

It was a scene right out of the National Lampoon movie *Vacation*. I was Clark Griswold, with Christy Brinkley pulling up in her convertible, checking me out. (And I was just as self-deceived as Clark Griswold that she was all that in to me.)

My two passengers were like, "I think that girl's flirting with you, Juan!"

"Yeah, it happens to me a lot in White Lighting." I replied. "It's a chick magnet. All these women, they kind of dig a guy with a fancy car."

Totally Clark Griswold.

I looked over again at my blonde admirer, and sure enough, she was checking out my car. Only I realized she wasn't looking at me thinking, "Hey, dude with the smokin' hot car! Pull over so we can meet." It was more like, "Hey, idiot with the car that's actually smoking! Pull over so we can put out the fire!"

Kim and Patrice saw what was really going on, and both started howling with laughter.

The car was smoking, literally. But I couldn't get over. I was stuck in the middle lane, trapped by solid traffic on both sides.

And it happened, just like I feared. White Lightning died—right there in the middle lane. We stopped, and the car wouldn't restart.

Traffic was going around us, and people were honking. I tried to play it cool. "Don't worry, ladies. In about 10-15 minutes, the smoke will clear, and she'll start right back up."

The women looked at me, dumbfounded.

The picture was really pathetic. I sat behind the wheel of this giant boat of a car, smoke billowing out from under the hood, at a dead stop in the middle lane of the Stevenson Expressway at rush hour on a hot afternoon. And there was nothing I could do but wait.

Traffic behind me got even more backed up. Drivers who were able to pass yelled the usual helpful advice you'd expect from frustrated commuters facing additional delays. "Hey, *#@! Get a new car! What's wrong with you driving that piece of @+*# on a busy highway?"

Others chimed in with the obvious: "Did you know you've got smoke coming out of your car?" *Yeah, I'm aware of that, thank you very much.* Or, "You're holding up traffic. Pull over to the shoulder." *Really? Silly me, I thought I was parked in the country. Now that you've shown me the error of my ways, let me magically move this one-and-a-half ton pile of motionless metal over to the side of the road so I am no longer an impediment to all you good people.*

For ten agonizing minutes we sat, scowling drivers passing us while I mouthed a pathetic, "Sorry!" to them. The women were real troopers about it and found the whole thing amusing.

Finally, after 10 minutes or so, I turned the key. This time, the engine started up. We made it all the way back to the office without another incident.

Looking back, I can make some interesting observations about myself. There was a time when that sort of embarrassing situation would make me angry, or even depressed. It would have told myself that I'm not good enough or smart enough to work in that environment. I would have had trouble showing up at work the next day because I'd be beating myself up for not being cool or successful enough to have reliable transportation.

Yet in that moment, I was able to laugh at myself, my crazy car, and just how ridiculous the situation was. I see now that I was gaining maturity. I was better equipped to handle the challenges that life threw at me—and even laugh at them. That was so different from how I'd been—and it was light years away from how my dad had acted all the years I knew him.

Today, since I can actually afford a good, dependable car, I can tell these stories and not feel any pain. But there were many years when we didn't have a decent car. After White Lightning broke down for good, I remember my in-laws gave us a used Chevy Corsica. It had all kinds of problems, too. We never had money to repair it properly, so we tried to have friends fix it. Instead of buying new parts, we searched for them in a junkyard.

The pattern with cars continued. For such a long time, every car we had kept breaking down. I was so often stuck on the side of the road. One time, there was a huge snowstorm, and I was driving back from the office with no heat in my car. My fingers inside my gloves were getting numb. The car died five times, each time blocking the heavy traffic behind me. Each time I waited, then started it up again after a few minutes.

In the cold weather, I always wore gloves and hats and boots in that car, and made sure my kids were dressed warmly whenever we drove somewhere. You never knew what was going to happen. Sometimes, it would take me three hours to get home from work—a drive which should have been about 45-50 minutes.

It's hard to look back and see how much my self-esteem was tied to my cars. I know that a person is more than his car, but I also know those cars did say something about me—*to me*. They said I wasn't good at handling the money I made. (We were terrible at budgeting back then.) They said I couldn't be depended on. If my car was unreliable, people gradually began to think of me as unreliable.)

I know having a nice car doesn't mean you're a good person. But when our situation began to change, I realized that having safe, reliable transportation was a good thing. I wanted to make it a priority. It was a way to provide for my family, and when my kids started to drive, it was a way to make sure they would be safe when they went somewhere.

Longing for a dependable car also helped me formulate the kind of life I wanted for myself. I didn't want a sports car, or some kind of status symbol that would tell others I was "somebody." I wanted a reliable car so my life worked smoothly; I just wanted to get from here to there efficiently. I was not trying to impress anybody or fix my low self-esteem with an external symbol of success.

I actually think that's what it means to be a good steward of everything God gives us in life. "Rightly-ordered love" is what theologians call it. The great church Father Augustine wrote many centuries ago,

But living a just and holy life requires one to be capable of an objective and impartial evaluation of things: to love things, that is to say, in the right order, so that you do not love what is not to be loved, or fail to love what is to be loved, or have a greater love for what should be loved less…

On Christian Doctrine, *I.27-28*

I grew up with nothing. It would be easy to think having a lot of material possessions would ease the pain from the hardships I faced, and take away the ache in my heart from such a messed up family. But that's not how life works. *The best things in life are not things.* It's OK to go after material pursuits that are worthy of your hard work. But don't do it to make yourself feel better about yourself. Don't do it to prove anything to anybody. Don't love the wrong things, in the wrong way, to the wrong degree. Look over your life, and make sure you have "rightly-ordered love" toward everything in it and every person God entrusts to you.

Because even the car you drive can be your teacher, if you're willing to learn.

Learning Lesson Recap
In life, we may have limited resources, but we should take advantage of what we do have to better ourselves. We must work patiently and diligently to improve our situation. What is it we want out of life? We must know that—and go for it!

Remember
Hard work is fueled by desire for a better life!

The hungrier you are, the harder you work.

(Proverbs 16:26)

12

Inspect What You Expect
to Gain Respect

Learning Lesson
Respect is earned!

I entered the doorway to my boss' office. He was seated, busy at work, but he looked up and motioned for me to come in.

I walked over to the chair facing his desk. I wasn't exactly scared seeing him, but I also didn't know why he'd called this meeting. He set aside the file he was pouring over and reached out his hand, which I shook. As I sat, I tried to ignore the slight flutter in my gut.

John Rante was well respected in our industry. I felt enormous respect for him as well. He was always good about getting right to the point, and he did so now.

"Juan, thanks for coming. I want you to know that I believe something's off, something's missing in your department. I need you to figure out a better way to work with your people." He wasn't loud or angry, but I knew he had serious concerns with my performance.

At the time, I worked at Online Data Corp., a credit card processing firm. In the early 2000s, John put me and another coworker as managers over a telemarketing department. We were trying to sell what we called an online application, a new product for our business. Using this tool, our customers could go online, sign up, and instantly get a merchant account—a credit card processing account of their own.

My co-worker and I hired a team of 10 to 15 telemarketers. After only a few weeks, we were seeing an alarmingly high turnover. We were disorganized. And our results were dismal.

Every week, we met as a leadership team with John and other department heads. My co-manager was the numbers guy, so when we gave our weekly reports, he'd quote all the sales stats. I offered "color commentary" my effort to make the bad news sound good. But putting a silk suit on a skunk doesn't make it smell any better.

John was utterly unimpressed with my song-and-dance as I made excuse after excuse. Yes, we had a team in place (revolving door notwithstanding), and they were busy doing…whatever it was they were doing. But they simply weren't getting results.

I could see the disorganization, but didn't know how to find out exactly what was wrong. I certainly didn't know what to do differently. This meeting was about to change that.

John continued. "So, tell me, what do you think is the problem?"

John wasn't just handing me solutions, he wanted me to think. I started with what first came to mind. "Well, we don't seem to be making very many sales," I offered timidly.

"That's obvious. What else?"

"Hmm. Well, lots of our people are coming and going, so maybe we're not hiring the right people."

"Maybe. Or maybe you've got the right people, and it's something about you."

It was hard for me to think that I was the cause of the problem. But I trusted John that he had my best interests in mind, so, if he thought I should look at that, I was willing to consider it.

John continued. "Let me ask you something. Are your people doing what you asked them to do?"

I paused to think. What exactly did I and my co-manager ask them to do? When we hired people, we told them how much we paid per hour and what their commission would be. We gave them a minimum quota and told them to meet that amount, at least. But we weren't really holding them accountable. We also didn't train or coach them on how to do their jobs successfully.

"I guess we need to take a look at that. I know they're making calls, but we haven't been giving them much feedback. I also think we've assumed they know how to do their job, seeing as they've all been in sales before."

"Here's what I know," John replied. "Clearly, you are a people magnet, and your team enjoys being around you. But it's not enough for people to like you—that alone won't get them to perform."

I thought back to all my work with youth ministry and how I coached soccer teams. I really loved those kids, and they could feel it. I gave them lots of high-fives, jokes, got them to like me and think that I was a lot of fun. I was full of encouraging words. But I didn't clearly define any expectations, and didn't give specifics. At church, the goal was simply, "Follow Jesus." On the athletic field, it was, "Win the game." But that's not enough in the world of business. My telemarketing team needed more direction; that's not enough in the world of business. (And as I look back, I'm not even sure it was enough for those kids, either.)

"I can see that, John. I guess I need to do more training or hire more carefully."

John agreed. "Those things can help, no question. But something is still lacking in your team, generally, and in your life as a leader, specifically. There's a bigger principle at work here. I don't believe you've earned the respect of your team. And you won't get that by being nice—though you'll certainly lose it if you're a jerk. Here's the deal: you have to find out what is really going on. *You have to inspect what you expect.*"

I could see the wisdom of that immediately. If I laid out clear expectations, that would help my people do their job. And it would be pointless to have clear expectations without also finding out how close we were to meeting them. Then, if I knew where things stood, I could help my team know where they stood, too.

John wasn't finished. "Let me go one step further. You need to inspect what you expect *to earn respect*. It's not just about getting respect so you can feel good about yourself. It's respect so your people follow your leadership. And they need your leadership to succeed. If things happened automatically in business, we wouldn't need leaders or managers. I'd just hire sales people, turn them loose, and they'd succeed. But it doesn't work that way. Your team needs to know you are there for them. They need to know you want something from them, and they need to know exactly what your expectations are. Then you need to regularly measure how close they are to meeting those expectations. They need to know where they stand. They need to know that you know where they stand. That might sound like controlling or dominating them, but when it's done right, it's not. People having respect for you creates productive and satisfied employees. And that definitely pays off when it comes to our bottom line."

I have come to believe that mentoring like this—where hard truths are spoken—is as much showing "love" as the high fives and joking around that I used to do with my high school kids at church or on the soccer field. I think in some ways, this is an even more valuable form of love. It meant John had to take a risk with me. He had to have been ready for me to get defensive. He couldn't be satisfied with me liking him. He wanted a better future for me, not just for the company, and that kind of concern is more than just using me for his gain. It is wanting the best for me.

John concluded our meeting. "I want you to apply that, and let's see how it goes."

The next day, my telemarketing team shuffled into the conference room. Several wandered in late, offering some lame excuse. No one seemed particularly enthusiastic or focused. They seem annoyed that we had called them all together for an all-hands-on-deck meeting.

I stood up to speak. "Okay, team, time for some hard truth."

I looked around, and in the midst of the sleepy, dull faces, a few of them were smiling, as if this was the opening line of a joke. I realized I had never talked like this to them. Why wouldn't they think this was another example of Juan's crazy humor?

I continued. "Seriously, folks, we've been pretty loose around here, and everybody's performance has suffered. So we want to make some changes. The first step is for us to get clear about our expectations. And here's the first one: you will need to make 100 calls, minimum, per day. And we will keep track of those calls. We will actually count them and take notes. From these calls, you need to produce at least five qualified leads every day."

Now they were awake!

It really helped that we had numbers attached to what we expected. As we did that, we could hold them accountable every day and every week. Whatever *matters*, you must *measure*. And whatever you *measure*, people know *matters*. Now everyone on the team could tell if they were on target or if they were only *close* to the target.

They could also know if they should start looking for another job!

I shouldn't have been surprised by what happened, but I was. Within about 30 days, four or five people rose to the top. Their performance soared. They were hitting the numbers, they were making their commission quota, and they were excited. When we defined our expectations, they respected those standards and began to succeed.

Another group of employees were not hitting their numbers—not meeting our expectations (which were now clearly defined). So we started working with them to improve their performance. When they didn't get better—and several didn't—we moved them out. That was a big change from how we had handled things in the past.

When we started firing underperformers, others took notice. *What's going on here?* they wondered. Almost overnight, they realized we were serious about holding them accountable to their quotas and results. By the time we started hiring new people, we had specific goals and specific targets we could lay out for them. We had a much better on-boarding process. And we had four or five people who were succeeding. They were setting the example for everybody else—to show them that it could be done and how to do it.

After a while, John set up another meeting with me. Only this time, we were doing what I'd call a post-game analysis. He made me figure out what I'd done right. He said, "Juan, as I told you before, your people need to know exactly what you expect from them. I want you to see that the first big change you made was doing a better job training people. That's a big part of what led to your success. You also started spelling out your vision, and you made your expectations crystal clear. Can you see how different that is from the way you were working before? You know what you're trying to do, and you've communicated that vision to your team. You get it. They get it. And now we're all getting it—a better bottom line."

To have my CEO identify what I was doing right and to sit down with me and explain why I was succeeding really fired me up!

And I needed that extra enthusiasm for the challenge John was about to give me.

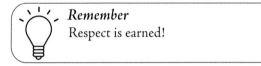

Learning Lesson Recap
If we want respect, it starts with us. We must work on ourselves and become a person people want to follow. It also means we have to be willing to do the hard things. Sometimes, people may not like what we have to say. To earn respect, we must set clear expectations and then hold people accountable for those expectations. When we change, things change.

Remember
Respect is earned!

So don't bother correcting mockers; they will only hate you.
But correct the wise, and they will love you.

(Proverbs 9:8, NLT)

13

What Makes the Difference

Learning Lesson
We need mentors—and the humility to listen
to them!

IT'S NO SECRET THAT MY HERO in all things related to
living the best life possible is Jesus Christ. Among his many
qualities, he was known for his powerful story-telling and compelling message. He was clear: "Do you want to know what the
whole purpose of the law is? *Love God, love people.*" Another
time, he taught, "Do you want to know why I am here? *I have
come to seek and save the lost.*" He also got his followers ready
for what they should do at the end of his life by telling them,
*Make disciples of all nations, baptize them and teach them to obey
all I commanded.*

Like Jesus, wherever you lead, you need to be clear about
what you expect. You have to set people up for success by
training them and giving them the tools they need. Lay out
a clear vision of what you expect and what their part in that
mission encompasses, and then show them how to do it.

I had a lot of success over the years. It got to the point where
I started speaking outside our company in various conferences

sponsored by various professional organizations related to the credit card industry. I was asked to serve on an advisory board in our industry, which I did for almost seven years. I was the keynote speaker at one of the biggest events in our industry.

Whenever I speak, even now, everybody wants to know, how did you do it? How did you build what you've built? I always come back to this first big lesson prompted by John's coaching me: *Inspect what you expect to get respect.* In my words, I tell people, *Give clear direction, provide the right tools and training, and let them go.*

Eventually, I was put in charge of an entire team managing hundreds of independent sales reps. We were bought by another company, and they merged us into a different company that had about three to four hundred independent sales agents.

Our team went all around the country leading these people. We met with them, trained them, and gave them a clear vision. We offered those who performed well an incentive to stay and be productive for our company. They were grateful and produced even more.

Eventually, I was managing three sales support teams, supervising about seven or eight people on each of these teams. I managed those teams and all those sales reps. It was hard to believe that this kid who came from welfare and poverty and abuse could now be managing several hundred independent sales people nationwide along with a team of about 25 support people. I oversaw all that.

I want to say one more very important thing that you may have already observed. For this whole process of better leadership to work, you not only have to learn to lead, you have to let others lead you. You have to respect other people's experience and strengths, and let them speak into your life. You have to be open to their suggestions and not be defensive when they give you feedback and suggestions.

Over the 18 years I was with John, I saw him fire a handful leaders who were not willing to be teachable. I remember key situations, even close friends, guys I had worked with who were angry or frustrated with the way the company was being run.

And John was gracious but firm. He would tell guys who tried to argue with him, "Look, I can't have you acting like that or we're going to have to part ways. I want your point of view, but when I've heard it and made my decision, I need you to submit to it." Several of those guys weren't willing. They really felt like they knew better, and they chafed under John's leadership.

Some of my colleagues who left were really angry. Afterward, they'd call me and ask, *How can you work for a guy like that?*

When I'm coaching people, I run into this kind of attitude all the time. Clients will tell me, "You can't believe how ridiculous my CEO is." And I respond, "Really? Your CEO is that ridiculous?" And they tell me, "Yeah, he's stupid." So I ask, "Well, how did he become CEO if he's as stupid as you say?" They may have a comeback to that, but I've made my point: you're never going to get ahead focusing on the faults of those around you. You're going to get better only if you work on yourself.

I'm not saying there aren't inept leaders out there. You may be working for one right now. It's undeniable that leaders don't always do things right. Sometimes they aren't as good as they should be. Maybe in some cases, we do need to leave. But far more often, something else is going on. Far more often our pride keeps us from seeing what we need to change about ourselves.

One of the most difficult things for people to do is to make personal sacrifices and humble themselves. Being part of a team will require that at some point. When pride kicks in, we become selfish. That hurts the productivity of the team. We need to put others first and serve them in a way in which we can all win. For example, I've grown more secure in who I am, which has allowed me to serve others and become a better leader.

I recently encountered a situation that illustrates this principle. In this case, I was the leader, and pride kept others from taking my counsel. I was called in to consult about a leadership decision within another organization. They had a leader in place who was not a good fit for the kind of leadership required, and I gave them the bad news that I thought this person was never going to fit the bill. They listened to me, but they didn't take my counsel and kept the person in that position.

Within 24 months, other leaders had left, and the organization was floundering. They came to me and again asked for my counsel. I told them again, they had the wrong person in charge. And once again, though they heard me, they still didn't take my counsel.

It wasn't a matter of my ego being hurt. I was telling them the obvious. It didn't work then, and it wasn't going to work now. I myself had sought out counsel as to how to advise this group. My mentor agreed with me; they were about to make *exactly* the same mistake again.

Why didn't they listen? I found out later that they were being swayed behind the scenes and were basically doing things in their own self-interest. As a result, the organization they led suffered.

Even when I mentor others, I still rely on mentors myself, because I'm always learning. The person who thinks they've arrived and stops learning is the person who has to start all over again.

Leadership doesn't mean you don't need to listen to others. The bigger the leader, the bigger the circle of counselors needed. The more responsibility, the more you require outside input. Always keep learning. Always look for ways to sharpen your skills. Always stay humble.

Over the years, mentors guided me to a better future. Mentors could have guided that other group to a better future. But, instead, they chose to go their own way and ignore good counsel.

My mentors have helped me overcome my past. John first started mentoring me when I was in my 40s. In many ways, I was still a kid inside and felt stuck there. But he knew my story and tried to help me. What made John so great is that he allowed me to lead others and develop my own set of leadership skills. He said, "Look, I'm putting you in a management position, and I need you to manage people. I'll help you to learn how to do that." Then he let me make mistakes. He even let me fail. But we had a relationship where I was willing to learn. I was willing to come back and take notes.

When I started having some success, one of the things John did as a leader was go back over what happened, so I could learn. He'd say, "Great job! What do you think has made the difference?" We'd talk about what led to my achievements, and why I was succeeding. And true to that first lesson I learned so many years ago, it was often related to envisioning and training those I lead.

It's weird how, years later, I can compare all this to what Jesus did to mentor his disciples. He, too, taught them; he sent them out; he let them do it wrong—then helped them do it better. Jesus gave us a model to follow in order to train others. We don't have to be the perfect Son of God to learn from and copy some of what he did.

I've gotten a lot of recognition in the credit card processing industry outside of BluePay. John is a major reason for that. Humble leader that he is, John has also expressed his appreciation to me. He's often told me, "Juan, I realize that the recognition and the popularity you've gained in our industry has given our company recognition. The fact that you speak in so many public gatherings, and they know you are an employee of BluePay, does a lot for our company."

It's interesting to me that, even at this point in my life, recognition is important to me. It makes sense given my background and where I come from. Early in my life, all I wanted was to be "normal." I was satisfied to just pay my bills and survive. But today because of the leadership I have in my life, I've become more than a survivor. I am a person who wants to thrive and make an impact on those around me. I feel like I now have value and I have the ability to not only succeed in my own life, but to help others succeed also.

I've learned so much from John over two decades of working for him, but he did three key things that made the biggest difference in my success. First, John trained me to do what he asked of me—after making sure I knew what that was. Second, he tested me by allowing me to do my own thing—sometimes I failed, but I always learned. And third, when I succeeded, he celebrated with me and made sure I was rewarded.

Jesus also did those things with his disciples. Those are the things you can do with the people you lead. And those are the things I will keep doing.

 Learning Lesson Recap
Mentors bring us experience in areas where we fall short. They can help us both in our professional and personal lives. They offer valuable lessons, techniques, and skill-development to help us achieve our goals.

Remember
We need mentors—and the humility to listen to them!

A wise man will hear and increase in learning.
And a man of understanding will acquire wise counsel…

(Proverbs 1:5, NASB)

Section Five

Reflections

A leader is best when people barely know he exists.
When his work is done, his aim fulfilled,
they will say: we did it ourselves.

—*Lao Tzu*

If you think you're leader but nobody is following,
you're just out taking a walk.

—*Author Unknown*

I cannot do all the good that the world needs.
But the world needs all the good that I can do.

—*Jana Stanfield*

No one lights a lamp and puts it under a basket, but rather
on a lampstand, and it gives light for all who are in the house.
In the same way, let your light shine before others…

—*Jesus (Matthew 5:15–16, HCSB)*

14

Important Lessons

HAVING GOOD PARENTS is a great way to start life. They can teach you and train you and give you a good launching pad to send you into adulthood and success.

Problem is, most of us have less-than-perfect parents. And some of us have one or both parents who really wounded us.

So how do we fill in the gaps left by our primary caregivers not being there, not teaching us, or, even in some cases, doing us harm?

I believe there is a way. As you know, I had an abusive dad and a loving but minimally-skilled mom. As a result, I required significant help so I could live a full life. I could never get different parents or a different upbringing, but I did get what I needed to be successful.

I had mentors.

I've learned several important lessons from mentors, and I want to share some of those with you in this chapter. All of us have to build our lives with what we've been given. Mentors enable us to have so much more to build with.

Mentoring Lesson Number 1:
Learn How to Resolve Conflicts Well

I burst into John's office. "You will not believe what Hawkins did now!" I said. I wanted my boss to hear all the details about my co-worker's stupidity.

"Before you go any further, did you talk to him about this?" John asked.

"Well, umm…I tried, but he's not really responding," I said.

"What do you mean you've tried? What did you say? Be specific."

I cleared my throat. I glanced at the floor, then back at John. "He's just being an idiot, and you can't reason with idiots," I said, ignoring his question.

John stared straight at me. His face was calm; his voice was low and patient. "Okay, Juan. It sounds like you haven't really talked to him, have you?"

"Not exactly," I finally admitted.

"Then that is the place to start," John said. "Go, let him know what you're concerned about, and then just listen. Work to resolve it."

"But I know he won't listen!" Even as the words came out of my mouth, I knew I sounded like an whiny eight-year-old.

"OK, so then *you* listen," John said. "Don't accuse. Just ask him what's going on, and try to hear his side of it."

I paused and realized that would be really hard to do. But I also felt like John was right. I needed to take the high road.

John could see I was struggling. "Look, that still may not work. But it's where you start. And if you find the two of you can't get to a place of understanding, come back to me. I'll get involved at that point. But I won't do that until you've done the listening you need to do."

John helped me to see past my reactions to the path I needed to take. This was not an isolated incident. Lots of times I had conflict with other leaders, especially leaders of other departments. They had the same title or maybe a title higher than me, and they were having conflict with me. I needed to find a way to keep my temper from getting the best of me.

As I started applying this lesson—just a smart business principle—it occurred to me much later that what John wanted me to do is actually in the Bible.

Take the story I just related. In Matthew 18, Jesus taught a basic principle for conflict resolution. He said if you have a conflict with someone, go directly to that person, one-on-one. Don't gossip about it. Don't try to get someone else to tell that person what you want them to know. Do the courageous thing, and speak directly to the person. So often, that's all that's needed. We just need to stop being so defensive and take that first step.

Jesus went on to say sometimes that won't work. So, if the other person digs in his heels, don't give up just yet. The next step is to get outside help. Find someone who can mediate and steer the conversation toward resolution. A third party can often help people tone down the emotion or exaggeration that so often characterizes disagreements. A mediator can help people hear each other and clarify what is trying to be said. That person can also be witness to the conversation to make sure any follow-up discussions accurately reflect what was said.

This was the same great advice I got from my mentor.

By that time in my life, I'd come a long way with controlling myself when it came to conflict with others. But I still didn't really know how to resolve conflict in a healthy way. I needed to learn this skill because that is part of how leaders keep a company running smoothly. Mentorship guided me to become a better businessman. It also guided me to become a better man. The things I learned spilled over into helping me in my marriage and other relationships.

In essence, I learned to overcome my natural tendency to take the easy way out. I had to be the bigger person. A good leader steps out and asks, *What's the problem?* At that point we need to listen. We stay engaged and don't react, even if the other person criticizes us.

Because of how I grew up—because of my past abuse and insecurities—the minute I thought someone was finding fault with me, I pulled out my verbal sword of self-defense (sarcasm) and started swinging. My temper was in charge. I created a lot of damage from that, so I also learned to do the complete opposite: run and hide. I got to the point in my life that I hated conflict. I wanted nothing to do with it. So it was a big deal to find a different way to handle conflict, without the drama and without avoiding it altogether.

Mentoring Lesson Number 2: Get the Data, then Make a Decision

I went to seek advice from Rex Roth, another mentor of mine, because I wanted input from someone outside of my work. Rex was retired with over 50 years of business experience. He also pastored churches for sixty years and started one of the largest Christian high schools in the state of Illinois. He's still my spiritual mentor, and I call him every week. We also have lunch together every month.

Rex taught me about good decision-making. He explained the need to not spend too much time analyzing something if all that mental gyration was just postponing making a decision. By all means, get the data you need. Then make a decision and keep things moving.

Given my background, this did not come naturally to me. My childhood had been chaotic. In our family, we did things by the seat of our pants. I never saw methodical, wise decision-making. No one ever modeled that for me, and I spent my early years muddling through as best I could with almost no planning and forethought. I put off decisions as long as I could—procrastination was my default. When I had to decide something, it was usually without much to go on other than my gut.

So I went into meetings unprepared, thinking we would just wing it.

In a meeting, someone might ask, "What do you think, Juan?" I'd ramble on with some stupid, made-up-on-the-spot answer. Everyone saw right through that. At times, someone would confront me: "Juan, get to the point." And, man, was that embarrassing.

I went back to Rex for advice. He said, "Look. You can't afford to sit in those meetings and not give input. You also have to bring the team to some kind of decision that makes sense. The only way you're going to do that is by preparing for those meetings. I don't care how busy you are. You're a leader, and you need to prepare like a leader, discuss matters like a leader, and then decide like a leader."

It's easy to say we're busy or don't have time. But we find the time for what matters.

Rex continued, "Look, you need to gather data. And you need to be clear on what the situation is. What is the issue? What are the options? What will be the consequences of each option? You need to have that information before you go into a meeting."

My decisions revealed that I ran things however I felt in the moment. But I needed to think about what we should do to move the company forward. And, personally, as a Christian, I knew I needed to pray about it, too. Ever since my early teens, I wanted to depend on God to guide my life. One way to do that is to spend time praying—both to bring God's wisdom to my decision-making and bring his power to bear on the outcome.

So to prepare for a meeting, Rex challenged me to do my homework. He'd say, "Look, you have to gather that information, evaluate it, think through it, and, then, make a quality decision. And on top of that, you've got to live with that decision. It doesn't mean you can't revise the plan after you've set things in motion. But you have to make sure that you're confident going into it—that it has a good chance of succeeding. Any time you make a decision and then second-guess yourself, you lose leadership effectiveness."

Looking back, I see that, as I began to learn this, I moved up the ladder in the company. From early on in my career, I was included in leadership meetings with all the other vice presidents even though I was just a manager. When I first started going to those meetings, they would all talk about company matters, and I would sit back. Partly because I was in awe of the calibre of people I worked with and partly because I hadn't done my homework, I was mostly a spectator.

I now realized my opinion mattered. I had to be prepared. I had to come into every meeting ready to give input and help the team make a quality decision.

I agreed and started preparing. And very quickly, my "stock" in everybody's eyes started to rise.

I've seen this mistake happen with others in business. Leaders walk into meetings unprepared, and they pay for it. They rely on their position instead of finding out what they need to know. As a result, they make questionable decisions and lose the respect of those who follow them.

A top leader will not accept that kind of behavior from anyone on their team. People at higher levels expect input and thoughtful decisions.

Rex taught me not only to prepare, but also how to evaluate the situation in order to make the best decision possible. I established a habit of doing that because of the way he coached me.

Last, Rex encouraged me to always pray. I am unashamedly a man of faith—a man who knows his limits and continually seeks guidance from God in decisions big and small. I found that praying about decisions and then listening for any promptings from God was also a great help in the process. The Bible says, "Commit to the LORD whatever you do, and he will establish your plans" (Proverbs 16:3). I became more intentional about doing *that* preparation for meetings as well.

As time went on, those manager meetings became places where I shared my point of view with more confidence. I brought value to the meetings because I knew what I was talking about.

The conversation in meetings where we talked about acquisitions sounded very different. When we were asked as a team, "So do you guys agree that we should buy this new company based on the data?" our discussions sounded like this:

First VP: "I don't like it."

Next VP: "Yes, I like it."

Then I would be asked: "Juan, what do you think?"

"I like it. I like how they're positioned in this particular market, and I like that they have the right leadership. Plus their expertise fits well with our existing technology." I had done my research. I had made a contribution with specific information that was for the good of our company, not my ego.

I would receive smiles. "Thank you, Juan. Good work."

The student had learned his lesson!

Mentoring Lesson Number 3:
Accept Criticism Well

I never had a problem listening to other people's opinions—as long as they agreed with mine!

Truth is, I was terrible at giving people space to disagree with me. I was even worse when they criticized me. Because of my upbringing, I was a baby in this area of personal development. I would come up with an idea or even make a decision, and, then if someone disagreed, I felt rejected. I consistently took their feedback as attacks—and, frankly, my immature reactions were very unprofessional.

But I also struggled with this in my personal life, not just work. This was a common theme in my life that affected my wife, my kids, and my friends.

I struggled when one or two people saw things differently than I did and spoke up about it. As soon as someone questioned me or outright rejected my idea—especially if a second or a third person jumped into the conversation—I would literally pout like a little boy who didn't get his way.

At that point, I shut down. I took it personally and closed myself to the discussion. I felt totally rejected. I felt like I was bad or stupid. For me, my ideas weren't ideas; they were part of me, an extension of my worth. So to reject my idea was to reject me. When this happened to me at work, it hurt me deeply.

I learned another success principle. As a leader, when I came up with an idea, or I made a decision, I needed to stay engaged. I needed to stop closing myself off—pouting in the corner or feeling sorry for myself. Leaders come up with the ideas and decisions, and when people challenge them, effective leaders listen and interact and welcome the feedback. Strong leaders don't pull away, and they don't criticize people when they have a different point of view.

I needed to change because my sarcasm was out of control in those settings. I used it as a defense mechanism. If silence wasn't working, I knew how to lay on the sarcasm and make fun of somebody.

Growing up, I perfected my wit—it was a reliable ally I often called upon when I was with other people. My humor made people laugh. Their laughter made me feel like they liked me, and that felt good. But I often took joking too far. I got people to laugh at somebody as a way to put that person down, to make that person feel inferior and under my power.

At times, I really let myself go; it was not uncommon for me to cross over the line from being funny to being abusive.

Several times in our meetings, I got glares from John. He wouldn't say anything, but he looked at me sharply and his expression told me, You need to stop right now. And that was enough to get me to shut up.

I saw that my tone in meetings was way off. It was clear that was not acceptable in corporate America. I had to stop mimicking or mocking people. Sarcasm didn't work. It only made people more defensive.

In time, I learned not to take people's reactions so personally. I began to appreciate having some "loyal opposition" in meetings. I saw people could still be "for me" when they were against my ideas. People could disagree, and that was not the same as rejecting me as a person. They weren't bad just because they saw things differently, and I didn't have to force them to see things my way (or put them down if they didn't). As long as they were cooperative after the discussion was over, I could see them as valuable members of the team and not "the enemy." And my responses needed to always be respectful even if I felt attacked.

This lesson helped me at work, but it profoundly changed so much for me at home with my wife and kids. Friendships have also grown because I learned to accept criticism well.

No one has all the knowledge they need. The path to success is lined with people you invite into your life who reach out a hand and pull you forward. Eventually, with their help and your hard work, you'll end up where you want to be. And then you'll reach out your hand to help others on their journey.

Today, I'm so thankful for mentorship in my life. I did so many things wrong, but my mentors stuck with me. And I guess what is also important is that I was teachable. I sincerely wanted to learn. Real life examples showed me a better way to relate to people in my world.

Mentoring me was a lot of work. But without these mentors I would not be the person I am today. They showed me I was worth it. Most of the time, I know I am worth it, too.

15

Pillars, Part 1

I've done things I regret. I share some of those regrets in hopes people can learn from my mistakes. I've also done silly things that make for funny stories to tell, and I love to make people laugh. And every now and then, I've left my comfort zone and been willing to change and take risks that have paid off. I'm proud to tell others about those hard choices that may have cost me something in the short run but led to the really good life I now have. In the end, whatever happened to me or through me, I love to inspire people with my stories.

But inspiration alone is not enough. So I want to share six practices I continually return to that are the bedrock of my life. They explain my success. They are the key pillars supporting all my activities. God is still using them to help form me into the man he wants me to be and I want me to be.

Because you've read this far, you know my story and have seen these in action (even if I didn't spell them out for you). Now I want to name and unpack them to help you see how they might help you.

The six pillars are:
+ Dream Big
+ Get Mentors
+ Set Goals
+ Work a Plan
+ Take Action
+ Serve Others

When people ask me, "What worked for you?" I share these "secrets" with them. All the stories I tell are ultimately about helping people do these things.

I told you earlier about my direct sales business. What I liked most when I saw that business plan was the emphasis on dreaming about what you want. That was how you were supposed to motivate yourself to do the business. My upline Gerry Betterman spent significant time helping me find a dream of my own.

Nobody had ever done that for me. My life had been about survival and what was the next thing that had to be done. No one took the time to help me think in terms of dreaming big dreams about what I wanted out of life.

Gerry asked, "If you knew you couldn't fail, what would you do? What are the things you've always wanted but never reached for because you were afraid you might not get them?"

"I don't dream about anything," I replied. "I'm just hoping I can pay my bills. That's about as far as I get."

"That's all you want out of life? What if you could make enough money that paying bills was never again the issue?"

It took me a long time to get past my scarcity mentality. But once I started letting myself build a dream, ideas started coming. At first, they were very basic. *What if my wife and I actually had a new car? What if we had furniture that matched and carpeting with no holes? What if we could actually buy shoes for our kids or take a vacation? Are you kidding me? That would be amazing!*

Gerry got me dreaming. Then he got me to focus that dream into a purpose, to have some goals. So, the dream becomes a purpose. It becomes a reason to live and a force that drives you to better yourself.

What's the reason you get up every day? What are the one or two things that you want to do more than anything in this life? Is it to run a marathon? Is it to become a doctor? Is your dream to one day have a car that actually starts when you put the key in the ignition? No dream is too great or too small if it's yours and comes from the heart.

Maybe you want to get in better shape. Maybe you want to be an astronaut. Maybe you just want to pay your bills on time! What is your dream? Do you want to make a big change in your world to make it better? Or do you just want a life with less worry?

Sometimes, you have to start with the thing that drives you crazy. What are you sick and tired of putting up with? What would life be like if you made change happen in that area?

Working with Gerry was the first time I took my dreams seriously. He helped me believe in myself. Going toward my goals forced me to face my fears. I found those threats and scary situations I'd been playing out over and over were way bigger in my mind than they were in real life once I confronted them.

First Pillar: Dream Big
It's the possibility of having a dream come true that
makes life interesting. — *Paulo Coelho*

Dreaming big is where it all starts. I don't know that I could ever say enough about the energizing power of having your own dreams.

Two verses in the Bible help me in this regard. The first is Proverbs 29:18, "Without a vision, the people perish." The original context is talking about God's revelation giving us guidance for life. That's the "Big V Vision" we need because, without God's instruction, we will waste our one-and-only life.

And I think we can apply this verse to the "small v vision" that comes from our own dreams. When we have a bigger purpose in life, it galvanizes our actions and gives us direction. Without a dream to reach for, we play it safe. We spin our wheels. We may keep busy, but don't accomplish anything. So we need God's Big V Vision to keep us on the path *to* life, and we need our small v vision to keep us on the path *of* our life.

The second verse that helps is Psalm 37:4, "Delight yourself in the Lord, and he will give you the desires of your heart." Notice the order there: first surrender everything to God, then your heart's desires will be met.

Delighting myself in the Lord was the starting place for me. I'd first done that in high school. But I knew I needed to re-surrender every day. I wanted to put him first and make him the most important "delight" in my life. When I do that, the verse then promises God will give me the desires of my heart.

What I find fascinating is that the Bible assumes our deepest heart's desires are good. If they were bad, God would tell us to reject them. But he promises that he will be the one to eventually satisfy them. Given that God is the one who created us, those desires must be his idea—our longings are hard-wired into our hearts by God himself.

True, sometimes our hearts can be confused and fixate on the wrong things. But the answer isn't to ignore or do away with our heart's desires. Not having any desires at all may be some people's idea of bliss, but it's certainly not my idea of a fulfilling life. My path has been to first surrender my heart wholly to God, then trust him to shape my heart and its desires into his image. As C. S. Lewis wisely observed: "…our desires are not too strong, but too weak. We are…like an ignorant child who wants to go on making mud pies in a slum because he cannot imagine what is meant by the offer of a holiday at the sea. We are far too easily pleased."

I want to go deeper and deeper into my heart and find out what God has put there. I want to fulfill the deepest desires rather than the superficial ones. It's part of God's plan for us to know our heart's desires, to understand what gets our heart beating fast. Unless he tells me otherwise, I trust that (other than reading my Bible and listening to his Holy Spirit) my heart's deepest longings reveal to me the things God most likely wants for me.

Dreaming doesn't mean you don't work hard. It doesn't mean you don't get an education. But unless you have a reason for why you're going to run this race, unless there's something out there that drives you, you'll never succeed.

You don't have to believe the same things about God that I do. But you do have to have your own dream. Maybe your dreams are only about materialistic things: a 10,000 square foot home or a really nice sports car. I don't care if that's the place you start. I think those things will get you going.

You may eventually realize, like I did, that once your basic material needs are met, it really doesn't satisfy you to keep piling on more "stuff." We all have a sense that accumulating material things is not what life is about. So deeper, more lasting accomplishments will eventually take their place as your next-level dreams.

But I am saying: start with wanting *something*, and go for it!

Second Pillar: Get Mentors
Leaders..should influence others..in such a way that it builds people up, encourages and edifies them so they can duplicate this attitude in others.— Bob Goshen

I've already talked a lot about mentors in this book. Yet I cannot overemphasize how important they are. Next to dreaming your dreams, this is the most important pillar I teach.

I find so many people try to go it alone. They want success, and they think they have to figure it out themselves. They view asking for help as weakness. So when they reach a roadblock and they can't figure out how to get around it, they give up. I was headed in that direction.

That's the wrong way to think about life. Of course you don't know what you need to know! Nobody does. You were not born having all knowledge about how to be the best version of yourself. You have to get that help from those you meet along the way.

Parents are the first set of mentors we have. Unfortunately, many didn't have great models. My dad wasn't there for me. My mom was a loving presence, but, so often as the oldest son, I had to care for her. Even if you have good parents, they can't teach you everything you need to know.

Once you leave home, you have the rest of your life to learn. The world is full of great mentors who can help you and teach you.

I think back to early influences like my sixth-grade teacher, Mr. Lowery. He showed me a completely different picture than my dad did of what man could be—kind, understanding, compassionate.

Friends like Tom Dowling ("T.D.") and Keith Cote in high school took me under their wing and, though they were peers, taught me about being a "normal" American kid. (And T.D. made me a fanatical University of Michigan football fan on top of that!)

Coaches, like Coach Rex in high school Coach Schartner and Coach Van Dixhorn in college, impacted me greatly. They taught me about responsibility, endurance, and godly values, not just how to play football or soccer.

My roommate in college, Bob Southworth, was about as opposite a person from me as you could be, but we became good friends, and he taught me so much about discipline and consistency. Kevin Olson was also a college friend who eventually became a mentor.

When I got into the direct sales business, I had Bob and Daneen Southworth who were my sponsors and Gerry Betterman who taught me to dream. Dan Smith was another business/life mentor who was the first one to explain in detail the importance of mentoring and challenged me to keep finding more mentors. He was my speaking coach. He was my life coach. He was my marriage coach. I can never repay Dan for how much he did for me. His wife, Betsy, was also a great counselor for Becky and me. And of course, I have to mention my best friend, Jeff Conrady, who became very successful. I ended up learning so much from him.

As I mentioned earlier, I met Mike Jakubik and his wife, Lynn, when I was in the direct sales business. To this day, they are two of my closest friends even though I live in Chicago and they live near Phoenix. Mike and I are so similar—especially our sense of humor.

Mike is also a great speaker. As we rose in the ranks of the business, we ended up speaking at many of the same events. We saw a lot of each other, and Mike and Lynn also started going to church with us. Eventually, we traveled around the world together to do speaking engagements. We've both been to England, Australia, and Hawaii together. He's an advisor in my life to this day. He helps me write my speeches and looks over my sermons. He's someone who gives me a lot of advice. Our kids are close and have grown up together. And we still talk almost every week.

So often, people think that they have no one who could mentor them, but they actually do. The question is, are you willing to look around you? Are you willing to open your eyes? Even more important, are you willing to *accept* help? Being mentored requires humility.

It's not that we don't have people in our lives who could teach us. The problem is that we may not be open to having mentors see our weaknesses and speak into our lives. We're too private and protective of our image. If we let someone mentor us, it can feel like criticism—and sometimes it is—but you have to let people know the real you, the problems you're facing and the things you don't know or aren't doing well.

Most people—particularly men—act like they are an island. Myself included, at times. We try to do life on our own. But we're missing out on so much if we stay isolated.

For many people from an abusive background like me, there's a "code of silence." Our abusers tell us to keep our mouths shut and threaten us if we don't. Silence is not about pride or vanity—it's about survival.

The one benefit of growing up in so much dysfunction is that I had nothing to lose. I started with so little. I had no false pride about needing help. So many times, I was desperate for it. I couldn't have hidden my needy side even if I had tried.

Even historical figures can teach us something. I was in a special reading class in junior high when I first heard about Abraham Lincoln. To this day, he is the greatest role model I've ever read about—next to Jesus Christ. Lincoln was rejected; he failed at business and politics; his girlfriend died; later, when he married, two of his sons died. His election prompted the country to fall apart, and he presided over a war that killed 2% of the entire country.

When I felt sorry for myself I thought, *Look at this guy. How did he keep going? What am I missing?* I couldn't read well back then so books weren't an option. Being raised in Mexico, my mom didn't know anything about Lincoln. I only got bits and pieces of his life until I was older, but what I heard really moved me. Now, my library is full of books on Lincoln. I've gleaned so much from studying him and his life. I even found a little poster that lists all of Lincoln's failures that happened before he became president. I keep it posted in my office as a reminder to persevere through hardships.

16

Pillars, Part 2

Third Pillar: Set Goals
If you want to be happy, set a goal that commands
your thoughts, liberates your energy, and inspires
your hopes. — *Andrew Carnegie*

THIS PILLAR PRACTICE most people readily understand.
They just don't do it.

Goals are different from "To Do" lists. To Do lists can get
you going. They help you manage your life and keep you busy.
But goals require thought and planning. They are about important things, not urgent things.

Most activities on a To Do list won't radically change your
life if you get them done. But goals make your life different.
They take you into new territory and shape who you become.

To Do lists are often do-this-to-stop-worrying lists. They
shout at you, and yell "Fire!" But goals come from dreaming.
They are soft-spoken and polite. You have to be still and get
quiet to come up with worthy goals. When you want to make
progress toward a goal, you have to get away from the noise of
what's pressing and follow a still, small voice in your heart. The
To Do list will object and tell you about all the people you're

letting down. Your goals will silently point toward a better future that's on the other side of a dark valley that looks a bit scary to cross.

Goals put down on paper are essential—a dream alone, unwritten, will not inspire or guide you. Adding pictures is even better. You have to make your goals vivid and compelling. Put them out where you can see them often.

I had a "Dream Board" at work. I cut out pictures from magazines of things and experiences I wanted—sort of a pictorial "bucket list." I had a picture of a dream home (not unlike the one I live in today). Every time I wanted to upgrade my car, I had a picture of the one I wanted, in the specific color. I had pictures of golf courses and beautiful islands all around the world I wanted to visit. I had pictures of different ministries and not-for-profit organizations that I wanted to contribute to, like Children's Hunger Fund, World Vision, Chicago Eagles Soccer Ministry. Perhaps one of my favorite images was a picture of a book by Coach John Wooden. It reminded me that, one day, I wanted to write my life story.

Every single one of those pictures has become a reality in my life. *Every one.* And when I reach a goal, I replace it with a new picture. For example, I now have a picture of some land that reminds me I want to buy a piece of property and build a training facility for young artists.

Goals must also be "Big Hairy Audacious Goals"— BHAGs, as Jim Collins calls them in his book, *Good to Great.* They also have to be specific with measurements, milestones and markers along the way so you know you're making progress. As someone has put it, "The moment you put a deadline on your dream, it becomes a goal."

Fourth Pillar: Work a Plan
Give me six hours to chop down a tree, and I will
spend the first four sharpening the axe.
— *Abraham Lincoln*

With your dreams clear and your goals written down, you have to devise a plan and work it. A plan is simply taking your goals and breaking them down into the action steps you will take.

This is not as complicated or hard as most people think. Take a dream like having a healthy body. A goal related to that might be to lose 20 pounds. The plan to reach that goal consists of specific steps:

+ Join a gym, and exercise three times a week
+ Research and plan out a healthy menu
+ Take a short walk every day
+ Break up time sitting at your desk every 25 minutes with 5-minute stretches and movement
+ Throw out all the junk food you have in the pantry so you are not tempted
+ Get help from mentors to put the plan together

The goal is "what," and the plan is "how." It's that simple.

Fifth Pillar: Take Action
Well done is better than well said.
—*Benjamin Franklin*

Research shows that if people make a resolution and then casually share it with people around them, they are 30% less likely to follow through on that initiative than people who set an intention, say nothing to anyone, and just go about accomplishing it.

That may seem counter-intuitive. Why wouldn't sharing our goals be a good thing, helping us to get accountability and encouragement from those we tell?

The human mind is a tricky thing. Apparently, when we talk about something, we fool ourselves into thinking we're closer to our goal. We feel just a little better about ourselves for having declared our intention. And then, we subtly ease up on ourselves and let ourselves off the hook. We are slightly less motivated to actually act to make the change we described.

The one exception is telling an accountability partner or mentor. Those people will actually spur you on and help. But blabbing about it does nothing to help—and actually hurts.

This may sound different than what you are used to, or may have heard. But even Benjamin Franklin made the point hundreds of years ago: don't talk about it—just do it!

This pillar is the antidote to those mind-games. When you dream your dream, set your goals, come up with the steps of your plan, you then have to make measurable steps. Make sure the actions you take are measurable; they need to have a "by when" attached to each of them. Put them on your calendar, just like any other meeting you have.

Breaking an appointment with yourself erodes your integrity just as much as standing up a client or missing your kid's soccer game. Don't do it. Write down the action step, and keep that agreement.

Sixth Pillar: Serve Others
Humility is not thinking less of yourself; it is thinking of yourself less. — C. S. Lewis

Think of the people you admire most. Not the glamorous icons the paparazzi follow around, or the "famous-for-being-famous" celebrities with their endless plastic surgeries and unstable, drama-filled personal lives. I'm talking about people with high integrity, people who are making a difference in their world, people with solid marriages, strong networks of friends, and a wake of worthy accomplishments trailing them.

They all serve.

Fame is fickle and frequently comes to those who do not merit all that attention. But people who make their life about helping others have a quality that is universally appreciated.

Your dreams may begin with you and the benefits you desire for yourself. I've already encouraged you it's OK to start there—especially if you've had a scarcity mentality or believed you were not worthy of success and the enjoyment of life it brings. There's no virtue in being poor if you are a burden to society. It's irresponsible to be reliant on others, constantly borrowing money and forever living paycheck to paycheck.

But I would not be telling you the whole truth if I did not say there's more to life than that. What will ultimately satisfy you are the ways you've served causes greater than yourself and the people whose lives you've made better.

People will not stand up at your funeral and laud the cool cars you had. No one will weep at your graveside because they knew you had an amazing house in Belize. Those who gather around you as you approach your final breath will be those you've touched and loved and served.

I think Jesus said it best when he cautioned, "What does it profit someone to gain the whole world and lose his soul?" (Mark 8:36). He was the original servant leader who knew what real gain looked like. He was the one who taught—and embodied—that "whoever wishes to become great among you shall be your servant" and he himself "did not come to be served, but to serve" (Matthew 20:25-28).

I don't think of this pillar as some kind of obligation. I've lived both the ego-driven life and the servant-driven life, and I have no doubt which is more satisfying. Hands down, I am most happy when I help people. When I see others thriving because of their interactions with me or services I've provided (even for profit), that's what gets me excited.

There's research on this topic, just so you know I'm not making all this up. When a study looked at people's happiness and the correlation between how much money they made and how much happiness they had, the results were stunning. Above about a $70,000 annual income, there was no appreciable increase in the amount of happiness the subjects in the study reported. It absolutely flatlined at that income amount and for all amounts above that—even into the millions of dollars. People did not have ANY more happiness. (See TED Talk by Daniel Kahneman: *The Riddle of Experience vs. Memory*.)

The study *did* show that below that line of income, people reported less and less happiness the lower you went. That makes sense, because as you go toward decreasing income, you begin to get into poverty levels and people definitely suffer when they cannot feed themselves or are fearful about not having a roof over their heads. Lack of basic material needs does increase suffering.

The main point to take home here is that *increasing* material goods does not predict happiness above a fairly modest level of income. It is simply not worth striving after exorbitant wealth because it does not—it cannot—make you happy.

What *does* give us lasting joy—a better alternative to happiness—is being part of a meaningful community. We are hard-wired to relate to others. Again, studies show the most reliable predictor of fulfillment and happiness is when people report they have satisfying, close relationships. And such relationships never exist without mutuality and serving each other. This teaching has been around for thousands of years, and it's being confirmed by science. (See "This 75-Year Harvard Study Found the 1 Secret to Leading a Fulfilling Life" in *Inc. Magazine*, February 27, 2017.)

I promised earlier I would say more about what I call The Core Balance System. As I build my life on these six Pillar Practices, I am constantly monitoring how I am doing. The Core Balance System is the tool I use to do that. It's like the dashboard gauges on your car that tell you oil pressure, engine temperature, or speed. These gauges tell you how things are working "under the hood" of the main areas of your life. When these are in balance, life works well. From time to time, they get out of alignment. That's when I work to get these all back on track so that my life returns to balance.

Here are the spiritual principles behind the four elements of the Core Balance System. It starts with "in the beginning." Those are the Bible's first three words. Because God made us and loves us, everything starts with our relationship with him. It really is the most important indicator. I call this gauge FAITH.

Then, God created another person, because he wanted humans to have relationships with others, not just with him. The first social relationship was that of marriage, and that is the beginning of FAMILY.

After that, God blessed the newlyweds and said to them, "Be fruitful and increase in numbers; fill the earth and govern it (Genesis 1:28, NLT)." He created a garden paradise and then told the first two humans to care for it. He gave them the raw materials, and it was up to them to manage well what God provided. Similarly, being good stewards in our day involves managing our FINANCES.

Last, we must pay attention to the fact that God made us with physical bodies, and they must be cared for. Just as we've been charged to take good care of the natural resources on this planet, we've been charged to take good care of our bodies. That care involves all we are, including our minds and what we put in them, our appetites and

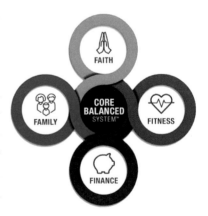

how we channel them, and our sexuality and how we keep ourselves pure from corrupting influences. This last gauge I call FITNESS.

I think the Core Balance System works best when you talk about these with a mentor, but you can use it by yourself. If you are mentoring someone else, it's a great framework for having meaningful conversations with them.

I close this chapter by talking about my dear friend, Dave Filkin. I recently hired Dave to be my life-coach. Dave was kind enough to write the Foreword to this book, and, as he mentioned there, we have been friends for over 40 years. As a life-coach, Dave helped me find balance in these later years of my life. More importantly, he's helping me move from success to significance.

Dave had me read a book by Bob Buford called *Halftime*, which I highly recommend. Through reading this book and guided by Dave's counsel, I am looking with more intention than ever at the next 30 years of my life. Because we sold the

Dave Filkin

company BluePay in the Fall of 2017, I have the freedom—in terms of money and time—to sort through what is next. I've come up with a few ideas and entertained a few job offers—even taking one because I thought I needed to do "the next thing." But Dave challenged me: "Why are you just jumping into something to keep busy?" I ended up parting ways with that firm, and it was definitely for the best.

I am truly on the threshold of the second half of my life. I'm focused on making a difference in the world around me—a *significant* difference. Dave has encouraged me to apply the principles in this book to accomplish that goal.

I'm still changing. Still growing. The title of this book is *Always Learning: The Juan Ortiz Journey*, which I'm sure you can see is true. I hope that what I've learned will help you do something with your life, too—something *really* significant.

Epilogue

Years ago, I decided to run the Boston Marathon. Frankly, I didn't take it very seriously. My training was almost non-existent. I thought, "If I don't finish, I don't finish. At least I can tell people I was in it."

Right before the race started, I knelt down to hug my boys. Steven and Philip were six and five. Steven said something that changed that day for me. He said, "Dad, I'm proud of you. I know you'll finish."

Those few words were like a jolt of electricity. Instantly, I had a reason to finish the race. I told myself, *I can't stop at 12 miles or when I hit my wall or any time; I can't give up. I have to finish this race. I don't care if I have to walk or if it's 10 hours later. I have to go the distance because my son believes in me.*

That's what a dream—a vision for the future as you want it to be—does for you.

My most important dream for my life happened when I was in college. I went to a Christian school that had chapel services every week. Picture me—the kid that the psych professor said was a deviant. I wore a trench coat and Adidas hightops, untied. I wore my baseball cap backwards. I didn't sit in the chairs on the main floor for chapel. I sat back in the bleachers way up at the top. My girlfriend, Becky, who is now my wife, sat up there just because she wanted to be with me (though she would have preferred to sit up close).

The guest speaker that day was Tony Campolo. He was this short, bald, Italian guy who spit half the time he talked. But he was mesmerizing. I thought, *This guy is amazing. What a storyteller!* I went from sprawled across three bleachers lying back with my hands behind my head and my legs crossed to sitting up, hanging on his every word.

I had no real direction in my life at that point. I was mostly doing what other people told me to do or expected me to do. I was scared of life and of the unknown. I didn't feel talented. Though I can't even remember the specifics of that message, there was something about what he did—the way he communicated. He was dynamic. He was funny. He was inspiring. He made sense. Listening to him made me want to know him.

I told Becky, "Someday, I want to do that—I want to speak to people."

And she said, "What? Really?"

"Yes. I want to do what he's doing. I want to be like him."

Becky knew how damaged I was; she saw my brokenness. But she jumped all over that. As soon as the talk was done, she grabbed my hand and pushed me down the bleachers onto the main floor. Then, she pushed me right up to the line of people waiting to meet and shake hands with Tony Campolo.

I was so mad. "I don't want to shake his hand!"

"You're going to meet him, Juan!"

"I don't want to meet him."

I was embarrassed, but she insisted I stay in line. I didn't want to have an argument with her—that would have been even more embarrassing. So we waited.

When I got to him, Becky chimed in. "This my boyfriend, Juan." I reached out my hand. I mean, he didn't know me from Adam. But he genuinely seemed interested in meeting me.

Just then, the dean of students who was standing nearby looked at me and Becky. "Hey, Tony is going to have lunch with a bunch of us. Would you guys like to come?" We ended up not only meeting Tony Campolo but having lunch with him.

I left lunch that day with a dream—and an example to follow. A seed was planted in me that has been growing ever since.

Keep in mind, the next day when I woke up, I had all these negative reasons why I couldn't be a speaker. *How could I get up in front of people and think I had anything to say? I'm not smart. I come from a bad family. My dad was a drug-dealing loser who treated me like the garbage I was. Nobody cares what I think or what I've been through. And speakers write books. They're authors. I was raised in a Spanish-speaking household; I didn't even speak English well until junior high. I never did that well in school. And on top of all that, I'm a deviant. I'm just a joke. All I'm good for is making wise-cracks.*

Do you have messages like that playing in your head? Am I the only one? I don't think so.

Here's the irony. All those reasons—those self-critical messages that I used to try to kill my dream that day—*those are the very things I speak about.*

My life is a miracle. God put that dream, that seed, in me as a sophomore in college. Isn't that crazy? For decades, I've been speaking professionally, which means I get paid. I'm a sought-after inspirational speaker. And I write books!

But I didn't write this for me. I wrote it for you. I know my story. I put all this down in print so you could see that if someone as unlikely-to-succeed as I was could make the kind of life I have, then you, dear reader, have a seed like that in you to make your life the kind of life you want it to be.

Find your dream. Seek out mentors. Make goals—put them in writing. Work your plan. Take a simple action step every day. And find ways to serve others—make your life about helping others, not building a monument to your ego.

Martin Luther King, Jr. said it best: "Everybody can be great, because anybody can serve. You don't have to have a college degree to serve. You don't have to make your subject and verb agree to serve. You only need a heart full of grace. A soul generated by love."